Summer Solutions.

Minutes a Day-Mastery for a Lifetime!

Level 6

Reading Comprehension

Nancy McGraw & Nancy Tondy

Bright Ideas Press, LLC
Cleveland, OH

Summer Solutions Level 6
Reading Comprehension

Printed in the United States of America

ISBN-13: 978-1-934210-46-8
ISBN-10: 1-934210-46-3

Cover Design: Dan Mazzola
Editor: Kimberly A. Dambrogio
Illustrator: Christopher Backs
Contributing Authors: Patricia K. Wyman, PhD
　　　　　　　　　　　　Mary S. Baird
　　　　　　　　　　　　Judith Backs
　　　　　　　　　　　　Chelsey Porter

Instructions for Parents/Guardians

- *Summer Solutions* is an extension of the *Simple Solutions* approach being used by thousands of children in schools across the United States.

- The 30 lessons included in each workbook are meant to review and reinforce the skills learned in the grade level just completed.

- The program is designed to be used three days per week for 10 weeks to ensure retention.

- Completing the book all at one time defeats the purpose of sustained practice over the summer break.

- Each book contains answers for each lesson.

- Each book also contains the *Help Pages* which provide explanations and examples of analogies, context clues, fact and opinion, cause-effect, synonyms, antonyms, and homophones.

- Lessons should be checked immediately for optimal feed-back.

- Adjust the use of the book to fit vacations. More lessons may have to be completed during the weeks before or following a family vacation.

Summer Solutions Level 6
Reading Comprehension

Summer Solutions Reading Comprehension, Level 6 exposes readers to folk tales, short stories, poetry, and non-fiction. Each lesson begins with a short reading selection. The questions that follow are meant to reinforce basic comprehension. Other reading skills covered in this book include the following:

- Sequencing story events

- Identifying the main idea

- Solving analogies

- Making inferences

- Predicting outcomes

- Building vocabulary recognition (Homophones, Synonyms, Antonyms)

- Using context clues to understand vocabulary

- Distinguishing between fact and opinion

- Determining cause and effect

- Recognizing an author's purpose

Help Pages begin on page 65.

Answers to Lessons begin on page 77.

Summer Solutions Level 6
Reading Comprehension

Lesson #1

The Fog

Katie awoke early on a promising September day. She flicked on the lights throughout her sleepy home, **cherishing** the quiet that comes before dawn. On these days, when everything about school was fresh, Katie hurried through her morning routine of bed-making, breakfast, and brushing. She snatched her perfectly packed lunch from the refrigerator, pulled on her backpack, and headed out. Katie needed to be in homeroom by 7:30, and she had always preferred walking to school. Getting there early gave her the freedom to visit with friends before the first bell.

Katie stepped outside and looked around. *Her backyard was as **foreign** as a distant planet.* Everything was **muted**, and it was hard to see very far in any direction. **Undaunted**, Katie moved through the backyard, just as she did every day. She couldn't see the swing set, though she knew it was there. *Gazing across the yard was like looking through a veil that couldn't be moved.* For a moment, Katie thought how exciting it was to walk through the hazy landscape, yet it was a little frightening at the same time. She had the feeling of being the only person on Earth. She could hear the sounds of invisible birds and far-off traffic. Moving through the deep yard, she turned to look back at her house but could barely see it anymore. She imagined traveling forward, but the ground beneath her became visible only one step at a time.

Katie started feeling a little spooked by her thoughts. And, what was that sound? As she turned to look, an **obscure** shape seemed to be coming toward her! What if it was something coming to hurt her? She was suddenly gripped with fear and the urge to run. In a panic, Katie began to move faster through the **murky** air, as the thing continued to come closer. She could hear a swishing sound and someone calling to her. Katie thought of her parents' warnings about walking to school alone and how they forbade her to go solo once the mornings began to get darker. She had felt certain that nothing bad would ever happen to her. But now, she wasn't so sure. Katie started running headlong into the haze, as the swishing thing behind her sped up to keep pace. Suddenly, she felt the thing pulling at her backpack. She gasped and turned to face the danger.

"Will you stop?" yelled her brother. "School's been delayed for two hours because of the fog!"

1. How does Katie feel about getting up early and going to school every morning?

    frightened   eager   sleepy   discouraged

2. Circle a word in the second paragraph that shows that the fog was not enough to stop Katie from walking to school.

3.   Underline the sentence that tells why Katie wanted to get to school early.

4.   Why did Katie continue walking even though it was very foggy outside?
     A)   She didn't know that school had been delayed.
     B)   She felt sure that nothing bad would happen to her.
     C)   She thought it was exciting to walk through the fog.
     D)   all of the above

5.   Katie's parents forbade her to "go solo" once the mornings began to get darker. What does it mean to "go solo"?

     A)   walk alone   C)   join a choir
     B)   take flying lessons   D)   play the piano

6.   A simile compares two things using the words *like* or *as*. In the selection, there are two similes which are written in italics. The first simile compares Katie's backyard to what?

          a veil   a hazy landscape   a muted vision   a distant planet

7.   Which two things are compared in the second simile?
     A)   walking to school and playing on a swing set
     B)   the back yard and a foggy day
     C)   looking through the fog and looking through a veil
     D)   being excited and being frightened at the same time

Underline a synonym for each **bolded** word. Use context clues from the story.

8.	**cherishing**	watching	awaiting	waking	appreciating
9.	**muted**	vibrant	subdued	clear	loud
10.	**foreign**	common	original	fair	unfamiliar
11.	**obscure**	unclear	harsh	obvious	sentimental
12.	**murky**	clean	needy	shadowy	atmosphere

Lesson #2

Bermuda

Each summer, I visit my grandparents in Bermuda. I travel by airplane to this spectacular destination in the Atlantic Ocean. Bermuda is an archipelago (a group of small islands), and the country is located about 500 miles off the coast of North Carolina. Many people might think that Bermuda is part of the Bahaman Islands, but it isn't. Bermuda is much farther north. The country has a beautiful climate with warm, sunny days. I always wear sunglasses and plenty of sun block whenever I am outdoors. It never seems to rain for more than a few minutes, although I have seen many vibrant rainbows. Rainbows are common because the atmosphere holds **moisture** arising from the ocean. My grandpa says the Bermudians always welcome rain because people in Bermuda use rainwater for drinking, taking showers, washing clothes, and watering their gardens. The buildings all have white rooftops, and the rainwater goes down into water tanks where it is stored.

There are lots of interesting things to see and do on the islands. One of my favorite activities is playing at the beaches. The beaches have soft pink sand which is great for building **colossal** sand castles! Swimming in the **turquoise** water is especially fun there. The ocean is so salty; I can float without even trying! The blue skies are speckled with puffy white clouds. **Snorkeling** is an amazing way to visit life under water. I look for sponges, brain coral, the most dazzling fish, and even lobsters. To get to other parts of the island, we ride in bright pink taxis. In town, there are gigantic cruise ships docked at the harbors. There's not much room for cars on the island, so lots of people ride around town on mopeds. But whenever I suggest a moped ride, my granny frowns and says, "No way!"

One very funny thing I notice in Bermuda is that the postal workers, businessmen, and even the police officers wear shorts! They're called Bermuda shorts, and the men wear them with socks up to their knees when they get dressed up. They even wear those shorts to weddings!

1. Which of these would be the best title for the selection?

    A) Building Sand Castles on Pink Beaches
    B) Snorkeling in Bermuda
    C) A Spectacular Destination In the Atlantic Ocean
    D) Rainbows and Bermuda Shorts

2. What is the best explanation for why the author's grandmother says, "No way!" to riding a moped?

    A) A grandmother does not know how to ride a moped.
    B) Riding a moped can be very dangerous.
    C) It is illegal to ride a moped in Bermuda.
    D) A moped is not meant for traveling on land.

3.   Write the word that best completes the analogy. (See Help Pages.)

     Bermuda : Bermudians :: _____ : Canadians

4.   Fresh water is not plentiful in Bermuda. Where do the people get most of their water for drinking, cooking, watering plants, and washing clothes?

     _____

Look back at the **bolded** words in the selection. Write a word to go with each clue.

5.   _____ swimming underwater with a breathing tube

6.   _____ extremely large

7.   _____ a green-blue color

8.   _____ humidity

An **effect** tells *what happened.* The **cause** tells *why it happened.*
Underline the part that states the <u>effect</u>.

9.   I can float effortlessly because the ocean water is so salty.

10. The sun is strong, so I safeguard my eyes by wearing sunglasses.

Underline the part that states the <u>cause</u>.

11. Due to the moisture in the atmosphere, rainbows often appear in the sky.

12. It is best to travel to Bermuda by air since the country is an archipelago.

Lesson #3

Water Cycle in a Bottle

Did you ever wonder where a puddle goes? Rays of sun shine onto the Earth's surface, and water **evaporates**, becoming **water vapor**. The vapor rises into the atmosphere, and then condenses, or gathers, in the form of a cloud. Water droplets in **clouds** form around particles of dust, becoming heavy. **Precipitation** follows. Temperature is what determines the type of precipitation that will form: rain, snow, sleet, or hail. Very cold temperatures bring snow. Warmer temperatures result in rain. Mixed **temperatures** – cold air meeting warm air – can cause hail or sleet.

Precipitation falls to the ground, forming new puddles, and some water soaks into the ground. Water is added to rivers, lakes, and oceans which are all forms of **ground water**. Again, the water evaporates. More clouds form, and then comes precipitation. The "Water Cycle" is a **cycle** because it has no beginning and no end.

How to Make Your Own Water Cycle

You can make a model of the water cycle to observe exactly how it works. Just follow these steps and enjoy a close-up view of the water cycle in action.

Materials:

1 clear 2-liter soda pop bottle and cap	a permanent marker
blue food coloring	water

Step 1: Peel the label off the bottle; wash it out and dry off the outside.

Step 2: With a permanent marker, label the parts of the Water Cycle (see below).

- Write Condensation at the top of the bottle where the cloud will form.
- Write Precipitation on the side; make little drops with arrows pointing downward.
- On the other side, write Evaporation; show arrows pointing upward.
- At the bottom of the bottle write Ground Water.

Step 3: Put about 3 inches of clean water in the bottle.

Step 4: Place 2-3 drops of food coloring in the water to make it more visible.

Step 5: Put the cap on tightly and mix by shaking the bottle.

Step 6: Set the bottle on a flat surface. Then don't touch it for several days.

1. The directions above are for creating which of these?

    an experiment   a model   a demonstration   a type of art

2. Why is blue coloring added to the water?

3. What is the beginning of the water cycle?

    precipitation   evaporation   condensation   none of these

4. Choose the word that best completes the analogy.

    autumn : Thanksgiving :: summer : _____

        Halloween   winter   vacation   Labor Day

5 – 12. Use the hints and words from the selection to complete the crossword puzzle.

Across

4. has no beginning and no end
5. a mass of ice crystals or water droplets that have formed around dust particles
7. what determines the type of precipitation that will form
8. water vapor turning to liquid water

Down

1. rain, snow, sleet, or hail
2. name for water in puddles, rivers, lakes, and oceans
3. liquid water becoming water vapor
6. water in its gaseous state

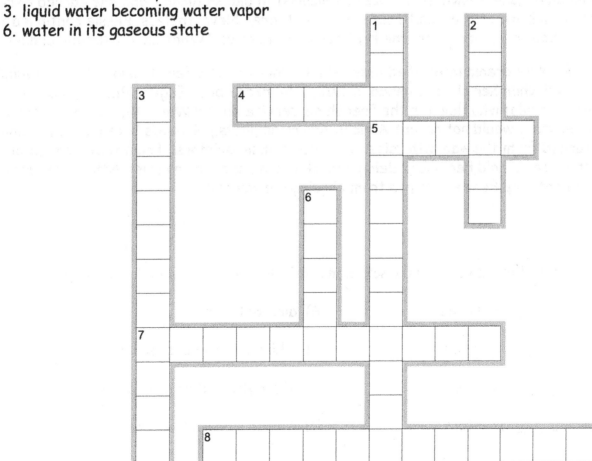

Lesson #4

Daring to Fly in the Face of Tradition: Bessie Coleman (1892 – 1926)

Part I: Chasing an Impossible Dream

Women did not win the right to vote until 1920, and back then, girls weren't even supposed to wear pants! Most people felt that flying airplanes "was not for ladies." African American women pilots were unheard of. But Elizabeth "Bessie" Coleman had her own ideas. From the time she was a young girl, Bessie dreamed of flying. She was born into a large family, and both parents were African American. But George Coleman was also part Choctaw Indian. When Bessie was just nine years old, her father made a difficult decision. Weary of the racial discrimination and difficulty of finding work in Texas, Mr. Coleman moved to Oklahoma where people with Indian blood had more rights. Bessie and the other children stayed behind, working long hours beside their mother in the cotton fields. It was during these times that Bessie vowed to make something of herself. She would gaze at the high-flying birds in the sky and dream of flying as free as they were.

Bessie returned to school as soon as her sisters were old enough to help out at home. She loved her studies and finished the 8th grade at the top of her class. After graduating from high school, Bessie worked as a **laundress** and saved enough money to attend college in Oklahoma. But her money ran out after only one semester, so Bessie returned to **domestic** work. Eventually, she saved enough to move to Chicago and join her brother, John. There, she entered beauty school to learn the art of manicuring. Bessie Coleman became known as the best manicurist in black Chicago, and she earned excellent tips from some of the wealthiest residents there. Nevertheless, Bessie continued to think about a flying career; she kept saying to herself, "What an irresistible challenge!"

Bessie's dream **intensified** after she learned about a female pilot, Harriet Quimby, who died when her plane crashed in 1912. She read about Eugene Bullard, a black American pilot who flew for the French air service during World War I. (Back then, the U.S. military would not accept African American pilots.) Bessie's brother, John, soon returned from the war with tales of French female **aviators**. From that moment on, nothing could hold her back! Being a black woman and a manicurist with limited schooling would not stop Bessie Coleman from chasing her dream!

Re-read the **bolded** words in the selection and match each word with its meaning.

1. _____ laundress   A) aircraft pilots

2. _____ intensified   B) a hired household servant

3. _____ domestic   C) strengthened or increased

4. _____ aviators   D) woman who washes clothes

5.   As a young child, Bessie did not attend school regularly. Why?

   A)   Bessie was not a very good student.
   B)   Bessie was traveling to Oklahoma with her father.
   C)   Bessie had to work with her mother in the cotton fields.
   D)   Bessie preferred to spend her days outdoors watching birds.

6.   Eugene Bullard was born in the United States. Why did he fly for the French Air Force instead of being an American pilot during World War I?

   _____

7.   In the early 1900's, most people thought it was not "lady-like" to fly an airplane. Which other careers would NOT have been approved of for girls or women?

   elected official   housekeeper   surgeon   seamstress

An **effect** tells *what happened*. The **cause** tells *why it happened*. Underline the part that states the effect.

8.   Bessie's dream intensified after she learned about another female pilot.

9.   George Coleman moved to Oklahoma because people with Indian blood had more rights there.

Underline the part that states the cause.

10.   Harriet Quimby died when her plane crashed in 1912.

11.   Bessie earned excellent tips since she was the best manicurist in town.

12.   Choose the word that best completes the analogy.

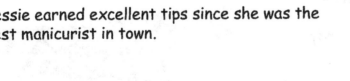

   Aviator is to pilot as _____ is to chef.

   food   cook   diner   servant

Lesson #5

Daring to Fly in the Face of Tradition: Bessie Coleman (1892 – 1926)

Part II: Against the Odds: Learning to Fly

Bessie Coleman set out to find a flying teacher. She met several white pilots around the city. They made racial comments and told her a woman's place was not in the sky. Several aviation schools refused to admit Bessie. Finally, she confided in a customer and good friend, Robert S. Abbott. Mr. Abbott was the publisher of a black newspaper called the *Chicago Defender.* He assured Bessie that her race and gender would not be such roadblocks in France. He advised her to learn French, save her money, and apply to flying schools there. Abbott wanted to support Bessie, knowing that "the first black female pilot" would make terrific headlines and attract readers to his paper.

Bessie studied French at a downtown school and found a better-paying job as a chili parlor manager. She combined her savings and gifts from wealthy sponsors, like Mr. Abbott, to cover the costs of sailing to France, where she entered a seven-month training course. The first airplanes were quite unsafe, made with open cockpits and **flimsy** materials. Back then, pilots were often called "flying fools." Bessie learned to fly a French biplane made of wood, cloth, wire, steel, aluminum, and pressed cardboard. There was no instrument panel. To steer the plane, the pilot held onto a vertical stick in front of her and operated a rudder bar with her feet. In June 1921, Bessie received her license from the International Aeronautics Federation. *Bessie became the first black woman in the history of the Federation to be licensed as a pilot!*

1. Why was Robert Abbot so willing and able to help Bessie?

    A) Abbot was a good friend to Bessie.
    B) If Bessie became a pilot, her story would help sell Abbot's newspapers.
    C) Abbot had plenty of business experience, and he was wealthy.
    D) all of the above

2. Underline three **synonyms** for the word *flimsy.*

    fragile   secure   weak

    durable   unstable   sturdy

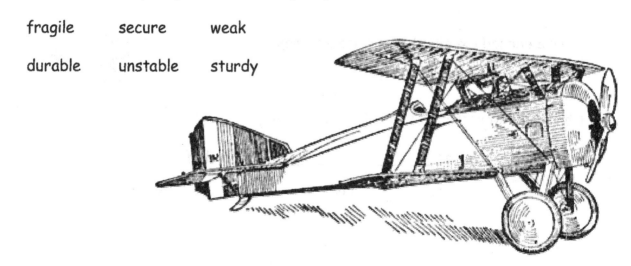

3. What "roadblocks" prevented Bessie from getting her pilot's license in the United States? Check all that apply.

_____ racial discrimination   _____ poor reading skills   _____ lack of effort

_____ shortage of schools   _____ gender discrimination

Write T for true or F for false (based on information in the selection).

4. _____   During Bessie Coleman's time, the French were more accepting of African Americans and women than white Americans were.

5. _____   There were no aviation teachers or flight schools in the United States during the early 1900's.

6. Why were pilots of the early 1900's called *flying fools*?

    A) Very little education was needed to pilot an airplane.
    B) The pilots dressed as clowns to entertain audiences.
    C) Pilots often played tricks on their customers.
    D) Airplanes were poorly constructed and very unsafe.

A fact can be proven. Write F if the statement is a fact; write O if it is an opinion.

7. _____   Bessie Coleman was the first black woman to earn a pilot's license from the International Aeronautics Federation.

8. _____   The seven-month training course did not give pilots enough practice with flying airplanes.

9. _____   The teachers who refused to help Bessie made a big mistake.

10 – 12. Look in the Help Pages for lists of character traits. Underline the traits that best describe Bessie Coleman.

    adventurous   introverted   courageous   arrogant

List three more traits that describe Bessie.

_____   _____   _____

Lesson #6

Daring to Fly in the Face of Tradition: Bessie Coleman (1892 – 1926)

Part III: Barnstorming Bessie

The returning Bessie Coleman made front-page news in America's black newspapers and some popular flying magazines. More than ever, Bessie wanted a flying career, but there were no commercial flights at the time, and no need for airline pilots. So, Bessie took to the air to perform for paying audiences. Bessie chose the most daring kind of stunt-flying, known as **barnstorming**. Barnstormers rented farmland for their shows. They would fly very low and then zoom high above the barns. They would even fly upside down or through the open barns to amaze the crowds. Bessie knew that she needed superior flying skills. Again, finding no willing teachers in Chicago, she sailed for France. After two months in an advanced aviation course, Bessie left for Holland to meet Anthony Fokker, a world-famous aircraft designer. She then traveled to Germany for more training with one of his chief pilots.

In August of 1922 at the age of 30, Bessie returned to the U.S., eager to begin her career as a performance flyer. At last, Bessie was ready to fly fancy loops and figure eights, pulling her plane out of tailspins in breathtaking feats of skill and daring. Bessie traveled the country and amazed her audiences as both a speaker and a barnstormer. She faced many more challenges, including some serious injuries and financial hardships, but Bessie never wavered in her dogged determination to fly airplanes.

At the same time, another famous female pilot, Amelia Earhart (1897- 1937), had her dazzling flying career. Amelia received global attention from the mainstream media during her lifetime, but the accomplishments of Bessie Coleman were not recognized until decades afterward.

If you would like to read more about Bessie Coleman and others, visit the biography section of your local library. Today, there are many excellent books that tell the astonishing true stories of pioneering women and African Americans.

1. According to the selection, why did Bessie choose to become a barnstormer?

_____

_____

_____

2.   In the first paragraph, underline two sentences that tell why Bessie decided return to France.

3.   Why do you think Amelia Earhart became instantly world-famous, while it took decades for Bessie Coleman to be recognized for her accomplishments?

   A)   Amelia Earhart was much older than Bessie.
   B)   Bessie Coleman spent too much time in France.
   C)   Amelia was white; Bessie was African American.
   D)   People did not care very much about female pilots back then.

Change the meaning of each sentence by writing an **antonym** for the underlined word. Choose from words in the bank below. Use a dictionary if you need help.

   bold   horizontal   courageous   safe   astounding   predictable

4.   _____ Bessie chose the most <u>daring</u> kind of stunt-flying.

5.   _____ Many excellent books tell the <u>astonishing</u> true stories of pioneering women and African Americans.

6.   _____ To steer the plane, the pilot held onto a <u>vertical</u> stick in front of her and operated a rudder bar with her feet.

7 – 12. Put these events in order by numbering from 1 – 6. Use information from the three selections about Bessie Coleman.

   _____   Bessie traveled to Germany to be trained by one of Anthony Fokker's chief pilots.

   _____   George Coleman moved to Oklahoma, leaving his family behind.

   _____   Bessie learned about Harriet Quimby and Eugene Bullard.

   _____   Robert Abbott advised Bessie to learn French and to save her money.

   _____   Bessie moved to Chicago and became an excellent manicurist.

   _____   Bessie graduated from high school and began working as a laundress.

Lesson #7

The Poison Dart Frog

　　The poison dart frog is a tiny creature whose **habitat** is the tropical rain forest. Most live in Central and South America, but some are also found in Hawaii. The **miniature** frog is only about the size of a nickel or sometimes a quarter; it weighs about 2 grams – about as much as two medium-sized paper clips. The poison dart frog gets its name from the fact that its skin is poisonous, and this **toxin** was sometimes used by Native Americans on the tips of blow-dart weapons. The brightly-colored skin of the poisonous dart frog serves as a warning and is used as a defense to ward off the frog's enemies. This type of defense is known as **warning coloration**. The frog's **vibrant** skin lets **predators** know that it is not a good idea to eat the little frog.

　　Poison dart frogs come in many colors. Some are bright blue with red legs and black polka dots covering their bodies. Others are yellow with black stripes and black dots. There are even solid green or blue frogs with black dots. Poison dart frogs live in a very moist climate. The female lays her eggs in a pool of water and hides them under leaves, protecting them from **predators**. Once the eggs hatch, the tadpoles must immediately relocate. Tadpoles breathe through gills and cannot survive on dry land. The mother carries the tadpoles on her sticky back to their new home. The tadpoles' new habitat is usually a leaf pool, high in a treetop. There, the tadpoles are safe.

　　Poison dart frogs in the wild usually live for about three years. But populations are declining, and the poison dart frog is an endangered species. Over the last 25 years, many frogs have lost their habitats as their lands were taken over by farmers and loggers. Also, many of the frogs have died from a skin fungus.

1. **Biomes** are regions of the world that have similar climates as well as similar types of vegetation and animals. Which of these biomes is home to the poison dart frogs?

    desert　　　　tundra　　　　rainforest　　　　coniferous forest　　　　grassland

2. Why don't other animals eat poison dart frogs?
    A) No animal is fast enough to catch the frogs.
    B) Eating a poisonous dart frog would be deadly.
    C) The frogs hide in the leaves of trees.
    D) Poisonous dart frogs are too small to be much of a meal.

3. Below is a list of factors that may threaten a population. According to the selection, which two factors threaten the poisonous dart frog?

    habitat destruction　　　overpopulation　　　competition　　　predators　　　disease

4. Underline the sentence in the selection that explains how the poisonous dart frog got its name.

5. Like all amphibians, the poison dart frog goes through the stages of metamorphosis. At which stage or states must the young live in water?

eggs   adult   tadpole

6. True or False?

    _____ Amphibians are born with gills instead of lungs.

Choose and write a matching word from the list for each of the terms listed below. Some words will not be used. Use a dictionary if you need help.

7. miniature _____

8. toxin _____

9. habitat _____

10. predator _____

Word List		
home	poison	safe
gargantuan	victim	ruin
hunter	diminutive	

Choose the correct homophone to complete each sentence.

11. The ship set (sail / sale) as soon as the storm was over.

12. The shoe (sail / sale) lasted only three days.

Lesson #8

Working Together

A father was tired of hearing that his **competitive** sons were constantly squabbling and undermining each other. The old man wanted to be sure that his three sons would get along when he was no longer around, so he called all of his sons together for a lesson.

First, the father asked the youngest son to pick up a sledgehammer and hit a target which was attached to a spring at the base of a pillar. The goal was to hit the target hard enough to propel a metal disc upward, and ring a bell at the top. The youngest boy tried as hard as he could but with no luck. The disc barely moved at all.

Next, the middle son attempted the task. He felt certain that his strength was superior to that of his brother. Even with all this confidence, the middle son was clearly unable to budge the disc. Finally, the oldest and strongest son came up to the platform. He tried **valiantly**, swinging the big hammer with all his might. The boy's face turned as red as a lobster, but he couldn't get the disc close enough to the top to touch the bell. The father smiled and addressed all three of his sons:

"Okay, my strong sons, now all three of you work together to ring that bell." The three young men huddled close and grasped the handle of huge hammer with all six hands. As they swung in **unison**, the metal disc rose to the top of the tower with great force, and the bell rang loudly.

"There, my sons," said the father. "You have succeeded. You've shown that when you work together, you can accomplish any feat. But when you fight among yourselves, you are like the heavy metal disc that cannot ever make it to the top."

1. This story is modeled after one of Aesop's Fables, which are always meant to teach a moral (lesson). Which statement is most likely the moral of the story?

   A) Cunning often outwits itself.
   B) Working together gets the job done.
   C) The strong and the weak cannot keep company.
   D) Don't count your chickens before they're hatched.

2. Why did the father call his sons together?

   A) He worried that the boys did not get along with each other.
   B) The sons were not very smart about business affairs.
   C) The father hoped to teach the sons how to swing a hammer.
   D) The information is not given.

3.   Which character traits describe all three sons? Choose all that apply.

_____ quarrelsome at times   _____ disrespectful toward their father

_____ half-hearted & careless   _____ determined to succeed

Change the meaning of each sentence by choosing an **antonym** for the underlined part.

4.   The oldest son tried <u>valiantly</u>, swinging the big hammer with all his might.

     fearlessly   timidly   shamefully   constantly

5.   As they swung <u>in unison</u>, the metal disc rose to the top of the tower.

     independently   unanimously   mightily   cowardly

6.   The <u>competitive</u> sons were constantly quarreling and undermining each other.

     bloodthirsty   aggressive   cooperative   reliable

Choose the correct homophone to complete each sentence. Find these words in the Help Pages.

7.   Empty the (pail / pale) in the utility tubs next to the washer.

8.   Emily looked very (pail / pale) as she glanced over her report card.

9.   The pants were too long but fit perfectly at the (waste / waist).

10. Turn off the hose, so we don't (waste / waist) any water.

A fact can be proven; an opinion cannot. Write **F** if the statement is a fact; write **O** if it is an opinion.

11. _____ Many hands make light work, but too many cooks spoil the soup.

12. _____ Reading one of Aesop's Fables is a very good way to teach a lesson.

Lesson #9

A Contest: The Wind and the Sun (A Re-telling of Aesop's Fable)

One cloudy spring day, North Wind was showing off to make himself appear quite powerful. He enjoyed watching people lose their hats, tossing them high into the air or rolling them down the streets. He loved seeing the trees dancing back and forth, sometimes bending nearly in half. North Wind chuckled at the children chasing their school papers which blew all over the place. Sun was watching all of this as she rested behind the clouds.

"I see you, Sun. You are hiding because I am much stronger than you are," boasted North Wind. However, Sun knew better. She simply smiled back at him, offering no reply.

"Let's have a contest," said Wind. "We'll see who can get that gentleman down there to take off his jacket. Whoever is able to do that is the stronger force of nature."

Finally, Sun peaked around the clouds:

"That's fine with me, North Wind. Why don't you go first?"

Wind huffed and puffed and blew with all his might. But the man just zipped up his jacket and covered his head with his hood. After a while, North Wind had to give up. He could not force the man to remove his jacket, and having blown out all of his strength, Mr. Wind felt very weak. He needed a rest.

Then it was Sun's turn. She moved from behind the clouds and shone her warm, tender rays in the direction of the man. He immediately looked up and smiled. Then the Sun burned more intensely, as her rays lit the bright blue sky. Before long, the man removed his jacket and lay down in the grass to enjoy the warmth and the light.

Gentleness and warm persuasion are more effective than bluster and force.

1. Which of these is another way to state the moral of this story?

    A) Kindness achieves more than brutality.
    B) Little by little does the trick.
    C) Do not trust those who flatter you.
    D) Appearances can be deceiving.

2. According to the story, why was the wind blowing so hard that day?

    A) A tornado was developing.
    B) There was a severe thunderstorm.
    C) The wind was showing off.
    D) The story doesn't say.

Does the underlined part state a cause or an effect? Write *C* for cause or *E* for effect.

3. _____ Sun shone her warm, tender rays in the direction of the man. <u>He immediately looked up and smiled.</u>

4. _____ Trees danced back and forth because of <u>the strong wind</u>.

5. _____ As Sun's rays burned more intensely, <u>the man removed his jacket and lay down in the grass to enjoy the warmth and the light.</u>

6. _____ The children chased their school papers since <u>they were blowing all over the place.</u>

7. _____ <u>Wind felt very weak and needed a rest</u> after having blown out all of his strength.

8. Complete the analogy.   water : tidal wave :: _____

   A) ocean : beach   C) ship : water
   B) wind : sun   D) air : hurricane

Personification means giving human characteristics to non-human things, and Aesop's Fables use a lot of personification. In this story, North Wind and Sun both have human character traits.

9 – 12. List at least three traits of each character. (See the Help Pages for a complete list of character traits.)

Character Traits of the North Wind:

_____

Character Traits of the Sun:

_____

Lesson #10

The Boy Who Cried Wolf (A Retelling of Aesop's Fable)

There were some villagers who were tormented by a vicious wolf that would appear without notice and snatch away their helpless sheep. To ease their **anxiety**, the villagers decided to employ a shepherd boy, as a full-time **sentinel**. He was told to keep the sheep together and under constant **surveillance**, as they grazed on the green hillsides above the village. The lad was instructed to alert the villagers at any sign of the prowling predator.

Early in the morning, the eager young shepherd arrived to safeguard his flock. At first, he was most **vigilant**. But after a time, the boy became lonely and very bored. Suddenly, he found himself yelling out "Wolf!" just to see what would happen. At once, the worried villagers ran toward the grazing land. They looked around frantically but saw nothing out of the ordinary, only the sheep nibbling peacefully. The villagers were **perplexed**. When they questioned the boy, he shifted awkwardly from foot to foot.

"I was just kidding," he said, "No harm done, right?" The **disgruntled** villagers simply shrugged their shoulders and returned to their work. Soon, the village below became quite alive with all the activities of the marketplace. The boy wondered if anyone would even hear him if he yelled for help, so the little rascal tested his voice again.

"Wolf!" he cried.

Immediately, the villagers appeared to help. They searched the area and counted the sheep, but they were **confounded**, as there was no sign of the **marauder**. The boy explained that he had been mistaken. What he'd seen was not the wolf at all, but just a friendly shepherd dog. For a second time, the villagers walked away and returned to their work. After a few hours the boy became very hungry. No one seemed to be bringing him a snack, so he decided to try once again to alert the villagers.

"Wolf!" he shouted.

The villagers dashed toward the meadow. But again, there was no **intruder**. The boy explained that he was hungry. This time, the villagers were quite irritated at the **ruse**. They harshly **reprimanded** the boy before returning to their work in the village. Later that afternoon, the shepherd spotted the nasty wolf prowling at the edges of the grazing area. He was sure of it!

"Wolf! Wolf! Wolf!" the boy shrieked. Hearing the familiar clamor, the villagers paused for a moment. They looked at each other and shook their heads.

"This time we will not be deceived. We have things to do," they said. No one ran to rescue the sheep, and so the wolf made a meal of the defenseless flock.

A liar will not be believed even when he is telling the truth.

1. Underline two sentences that explain what the shepherd boy was told to do.

2.   Whose fault was it that the sheep were attacked? Explain your opinion.

_____

_____

3.   What will the villagers probably do next?
     A)   Hire a different shepherd.   C)   Keep the sheep in sheds.
     B)   Put the boy in jail.   D)   Sell all the sheep.

4.   Choose all the character traits that describe the shepherd. (See the Help Pages.)

     conscientious   mischievous   reliable   foolish   troublesome

5.   Complete the analogy.   vigilant : careless :: frantic : _____
         watchful   calm   worried   lazy

Use **bolded** words from the story to complete the following items.

6.   Which word is a **synonym** for *worry* or *nervousness*? _____

7.   The wolf is called a "prowling predator." List two other names for the wolf.

     _____   _____

8.   Which three words describe the villagers when they responded to the boy's call for help?

     _____   _____   _____

9.   Which word is a **synonym** for *trick*?   _____

10. Which word names a guard?   _____

11. Which word is the opposite of *praised*?   _____

12. Which word means *close supervision*?   _____

Lesson #11

Vocabulary Review

Complete the crossword puzzle on the next page. The word bank contains the bolded words from previous lessons; some of the words will not be used.

foreign	muted	cherishing	undaunted	vigilant	toxin
obscure	anxiety	vibrant	confounded	habitat	archipelago
murky	colossal	intruder	moisture	rascal	surveillance
turquoise	flimsy	snorkeling	laundress	aviators	disgruntled
marauder	ruse	predator	intensified	miniature	perplexed
sentinel	unison	valiantly	competitive	domestic	barnstorm

Across
3. unfamiliar, unknown, alien
7. puzzled, confused, bewildered
9. watchful, attentive, alert
11. environment, home, surroundings
12. fearless, unworried, unconcerned
13. vague, unclear, murky
16. unanimously, agreement, harmony
18. trick, hoax, scam
19. poison, venom, contaminant
20. fragile, unstable, weak

Down
1. observation, supervision, close watch
2. aggressive, forceful, spirited
4. tiny, small, diminutive
5. lookout, guard, sentry
6. a group of islands
8. killer, hunter, carnivore
10. raider, looter, prowler
14. huge, enormous, gigantic
15. lively, colorful, bright
17. nervousness, worry, concern

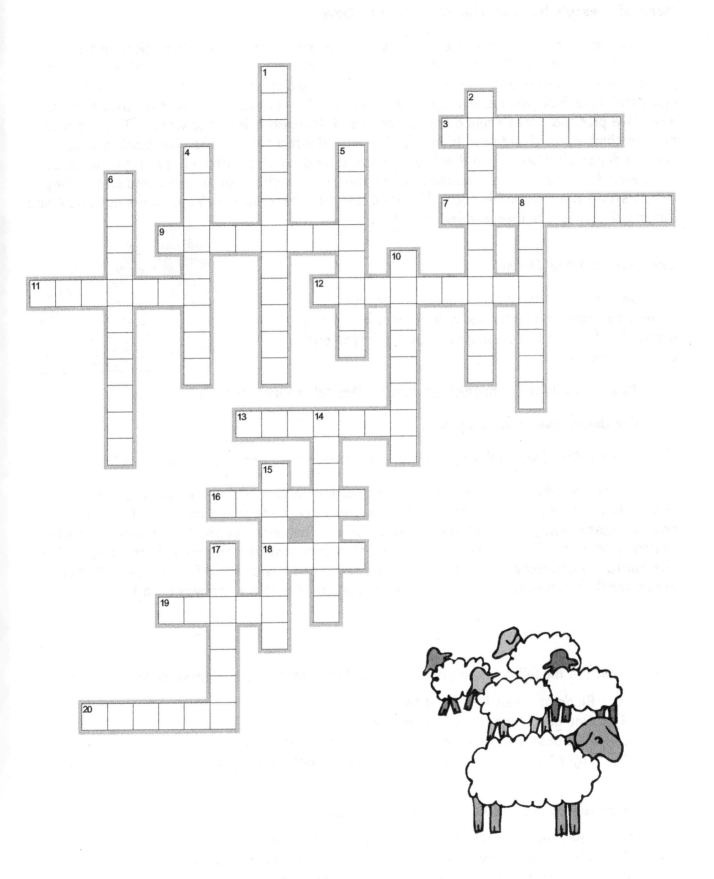

Lesson #12

More of Aesop's Fables: The Ant and the Dove

One day, a thirsty ant came upon a vast river and leaned over its bank to get a fresh drink of water. The current was rushing by so forcefully that the ant was quickly sucked into the water and carried away. Just as the ant was about to be drowned, a beautiful dove flew overhead and noticed that the little creature was in great distress. The dove plucked a leaf from a nearby tree and dropped it into the water. The ant was able to climb aboard and save himself. The leaf floated toward the riverbank, and as the ant scrambled back onto dry land, he saw a bird-catcher with a big net gazing up at the beautiful dove. The ant guessed what the bird-catcher had in mind, and so the tiny insect stung the man on his foot. The bird-catcher immediately dropped his net and cried out in pain, while the lovely white dove flew away.

The Lion and the Mouse

On a warm summer day, a grumpy lion was awakened from his nap by a silly little mouse running across his face. The lion snapped open his eyes and grasped the mouse!

"Now you will be my breakfast, foolish Mouse!" roared the lion.

The **diminutive** creature pleaded,

"Please, Sir, if you will only release me, I promise to repay your kindness soon."

The lion laughed at this ridiculous **proposition**! Nevertheless, he decided to let the **pathetic** mouse go, thinking that the **scrawny** creature would not provide much nourishment anyway. A short time later, that very lion was caught by some hunters and bound up in a net. The mouse was not far off and recognized the roar of the lion. While the hunters were away, the little mouse worked **diligently** at his difficult task. With his sharp teeth, the mouse gnawed at the ropes until the mighty lion was able to run free.

1. Which of the following might be the moral (lesson) for both of these fables?

   A) Birds of a feather flock together.
   B) One good turn deserves another.
   C) The best intentions do not always insure success.
   D) Injuries may be forgiven, but they will not be forgotten.

2. Why did the lion decide to let the little mouse go?

   A) The lion believed that the mouse would one day save him.
   B) The lion was laughing so hard, he accidently released the mouse.
   C) The lion thought the mouse was too small to eat.
   D) The lion was scared off by the hunters.

3.   Why did the dove try to save the ant from drowning?

    A)   The ant pleaded for help.
    B)   The dove knew there was a bird-catcher near the river.
    C)   The dove and the ant had been friends for many years.
    D)   The story does not give a reason.

4.   An **antagonist** in a story is the "bad guy" or an enemy to the hero. Which of the following is an antagonist in both fables?

        a lion   an ant   a dove   a human   none of these

5.   Complete the analogy.   bird-catcher : _____ :: hunter : lion

For the next three sentences, choose an **antonym** for each underlined word.

6.   The cranky lion decided to let the <u>pathetic</u> mouse go.

        feeble   pitiable   strong   wretched

7.   The <u>diminutive</u> creature pleaded with the powerful lion.

        small   petite   miniature   large

8.   The little mouse worked <u>diligently</u> in an attempt to save the lion.

        haphazardly   meticulously   conscientiously   alertly

9.   Cross out the word that is NOT a synonym for the word *proposition*.

        offer   proposal   suggestion   occupation

Which traits best describe each character? (See the Help Pages for a list of traits.)

10.   _____ Dove   A) dependable, hopeful, hard-working

11.   _____ Mouse   B) doubtful, grouchy, arrogant

12.   _____ Lion   C) kind-hearted, compassionate, quick thinking

Lesson #13

Re-worded Sayings

Every language contains many maxims, proverbs, and sayings, like the morals in Aesop's Fables. Below is a list of common phrases, but most of the words have been replaced with synonyms. Match each saying with its more common version. Some will not be used.

Example: (saying)   A single solicitous endeavor warrants the same.

          (common version)   One good turn deserves another.

A) It is better to give than to receive.
B) United we stand; divided we fall.
C) It is unwise to be greedy.
D) Birds of a feather flock together.
E) Slow and steady wins the race.
F) A bird in the hand is worth two in the bush.
G) You can catch more flies with honey than with vinegar.
H) Don't count your chickens before they're hatched.

1. _____ **Amalgamated** we **prevail**, while **alienated**, we collapse.

2. _____ Do not **enumerate** fowl in **anticipation** of their birth.

3. _____ Winged creatures of identical variety gather in **gregarious** groups and migrate **harmoniously**.

4. _____ It is possible to **seize** greater quantities of insects by utilizing a **saccharine** product, rather than with acetic acid.

5. _____ It is **injudicious** to be **insatiable**.

6. _____ **Measured** and deliberate **triumphs** in competition.

7 – 12. Now, complete the chart using the **bolded** words from items 1-6. Each line contains a list of words that mean the same or almost the same as one of the bolded words. A few have been done for you.

gregarious	social, companionable, chummy, friendly
	ill-advised, foolish, unwise, inadvisable
	agreeably, in agreement, in unison, together
	exact, unhurried, calculated, slow
prevail	triumph, win, succeed, overcome
	combined, together, in concert, as one, unified
insatiable	ravenous, unquenchable, voracious, avid
	expectation, hope, eagerness, expectancy
	itemize, list, detail, spell out, specify, count
	estranged, separated, not speaking, at odds
	succeeds, comes in first, prevails, reigns
	sugary, syrupy, sweet
	grab, snatch, get hold of, catch, take

Lesson #14

Insects, by John Clare (1793-1864)

A)   These tiny loiterers on the barley's beard,
     And happy units of a numerous herd
     Of playfellows, the laughing Summer brings,
     Mocking the sunshine on their glittering wings,

B)   How merrily they creep, and run, and fly!
     No kin they bear to labour's **drudgery**,
     Smoothing the velvet of the pale hedge-rose;
     And where they fly for dinner no one knows -

C)   The dew-drops feed them not - they love the shine
     Of noon, whose suns may bring them golden wine
     All day they're playing in their Sunday dress -
     When night **reposes**, for they can do no less;

D)   Then, to the heath-bell's purple hood they fly,
     And like to princes in their slumbers lie,
     Secure from rain, and dropping dews, and all,
     In silken beds and roomy painted hall.

E)   So merrily they spend their summer-day,
     Now in the corn-fields, now in the new-mown hay.
     One almost fancies that such happy things,
     With coloured hoods and richly **burnished** wings,

F)   Are fairy folk, in splendid masquerade
     Disguised, as if of mortal folk afraid,
     Keeping their joyous **pranks** a mystery still,
     Lest glaring day should do their secrets ill.

ripe barley

1.   Which statement tells how the author of this poem feels about insects?

   A)   Insects are part of nature, but they are annoying to humans.
   B)   Insects are beautiful and playful; they live happy lives.
   C)   Insects live short, dreary lives, but they do an important job.
   D)   Insects should be wiped out, so they won't damage crops.

2.   In Part F, the insects are compared with what?

   children on Halloween   elves in costumes   the petals of flowers

3.   What are *tiny loiterers on the barley's beard?* (Part A)

   A)   insects resting on the long bristles of ripe barley
   B)   fairies in the woods
   C)   bugs that get caught in hair on a man's chin
   D)   none of these

4.   What does the author mean by these words: *playing in their Sunday dress?* (Part C)

   A)   insects are colorful   C)   insects always look their best
   B)   insects are playful   D)   all of these

5.   Re-read part D. The author describes how insects go to the purple, hood-like flowers of a plant called heath. What do the insects do there?

   dance   weep   sleep   lay their eggs

6.   The *silken beds* and *roomy painted hall* keeps the insects safe from what?

   lightning   drought   predators   rain and dew

7 – 12. Match each word from the poem with a word whose meaning is nearly the same.

   _____ mocking   A) safe

   _____ drudgery   B) mischief

   _____ reposes   C) teasing

   _____ burnished   D) work

   _____ disguised   E) relaxes

   _____ pranks   F) polished

   _____ secure   G) masked

Lesson #15

Working for a Magazine

Job	Requirements (in addition to college degree)	Description of Duties	Years Experience Preferred
Editor	strong language skills; detail-oriented; knowledge of the magazine's content and style	read and revise articles; approve layouts, graphics and photos, and all other content	12
Art Director	experience in publishing; strong visual skills; knowledge of magazine's content and style	responsible for the overall visual "style" of the magazine; oversees graphic designers	8
Staff writer	knowledge of magazine's content; strong language skills	write content for the magazine; work with editors to make sure each article is great	5
Graphic Designer	a strong portfolio; strong visual skills; detail-oriented; knowledge of the magazine's style	design layouts (arrange text, graphics, and photos); work with editing department	5
Photographer	a strong portfolio; strong visual skills; knowledge of the magazine's style	take photos for the cover and photos to accompany articles; report to art director	3

1. What would be the best title for the informational table above?

    A)   Professional Careers for College Grads
    B)   Going to College for Graphic Design
    C)   Becoming a Professional Publisher
    D)   Careers in Magazine Publishing

2. Which professional would work most closely with staff writers to make sure that articles are well written and error-free?

    art director   editor   photographer   graphic designer

3.   Who is responsible for arranging the photos to accompany each article?

   art director   editor   staff writer   graphic designer

4.   Who is most likely the one who supervises staff writers?

   art director   sales rep   editor   photographer

5.   A **portfolio** is a collection of samples of a person's best work. Which members of the staff must have strong portfolios?

   art director   graphic designer   sales representative

   editor   staff writer   photographer

6.   Complete the analogy.

   computer : writer :: _____ : photographer

Read each statement. Write F if it is a fact or O if it is an opinion.

7.   _____   A photographer is trained to take photos for a number of different applications.

8.   _____   A college degree and five years of experience will make a staff writer very good at his job.

9.   _____   An editor's job is most important and should have the highest pay.

Sometimes a statement includes both fact and opinion. Underline the part of each sentence that states a <u>fact</u>.

10.   The publishing world is highly competitive, and most jobs require a college degree.

11.   Although the best jobs go to people who speak multiple languages, there are many different careers that require strong language skills.

12.   The graphic designer works with both text and art, so she will enjoy her work more if she is given complete artistic freedom.

Lesson #16

The Roller Coaster Ride

Simon and his family loved to go to amusement parks, although Simon never took pleasure in roller coasters the way the rest of his family did. Mom, Dad, Kenny, and Liz all looked forward to trying out the newest and biggest coasters at every park the family visited. But to Simon, roller coasters were too loud – and too fast – and a little scary. His parents were constantly telling him how much fun coaster rides were, but Simon could not imagine the fun. It would be more like torture to ride up steep hills, only to race back down, flipping over and speeding through double loops. His older brother and sister called him a baby, but Simon knew that he was just being sensible.

One warm summer day, Simon's parents tried once again to convince him that if he would just try one roller coaster ride, he would probably love it. Simon watched as kids climbed out of the cars at the end of the coaster rides. They seemed breathlessly happy, and lots of kids were getting right back in line to ride again. Some of the adults staggered around a little as they exited the ramps, but they were all smiling. Simon thought about getting on the coaster just to make everyone happy, but he was really afraid. At this particular park, there was an older roller coaster; it didn't climb as high as the newer ones did. And there was no turning upside-down. Simon finally agreed to get on this ride with his parents. As they stood in the long line, Simon watched each car go up-and-down, up-and-around, and down one last time. It really didn't last very long at all. The line moved quickly, and as they drew closer, Simon could hear the rickety coaster pulling cars slowly up the first hill. The old coaster was made of wood, so it was noisier than the others. People were screaming as the cars careened around a wide bend and down the other side of the hill. Hearing the clamor, Simon reasoned that his parents would not ever put him in danger. He knew that he probably wouldn't die and kept telling himself everything would be okay.

Soon, it was their turn to ride the wobbly monster. As he stood on the platform waiting to get onboard, Simon suddenly felt calm. He was going to really enjoy riding this roller coaster. Maybe he would ride every coaster in the park that day! A car stopped where Simon and his parents were standing. They had planned to sit in the middle section for Simon's first ride. Simon's dad climbed into the car, sat down, and buckled himself in. Then, his mom got in, sat on the other side, and fastened her seatbelt. Simon was going to sit between them. Mom looked up at Simon, smiled, and patted the seat next to her. Simon took a deep breath and stepped over his mother and into the car. Then, he stepped over his father onto the platform. The car began its sluggish ascent, as Simon headed toward the exit ramp. Without looking back, he skipped down the steps. Then Simon watched as his parents enjoyed the minute-long ride of a lifetime!

1. According to the story, who tried to convince Simon to ride a roller coaster?

    his brother   his sister   his friends   his parents   all of these

2. Why did Simon feel that it was not sensible for him to ride roller coasters?

   A) He heard a news report that claimed roller coasters were not safe.
   B) Simon got very dizzy and sick on roller coaster rides.
   C) He was afraid of riding roller coasters.
   D) all of these

3. Why did Simon's parents suggest he try the older roller coaster?

   A) The ride was slower, and the tracks were made of wood.
   B) The line to get on the old coaster moved very quickly.
   C) The coaster didn't flip the rider upside-down.
   D) The older coaster was much quieter and there was no screaming.

4. What finally convinced Simon that he would be okay on the roller coaster ride?

   A) He was tired of being called a baby.
   B) He wanted to make everyone happy.
   C) He knew his parents would not let him get hurt.
   D) He saw other people having fun on the ride.

5. It wasn't until the very last minute that Simon decided not to ride the coaster. Underline two sentences in the last paragraph that let the reader know this.

Cause and Effect: Underline the part of the sentence that states a cause.

6. The old coaster was made of wood, so it was noisier than the others.

7. Simon's siblings called him a baby because he refused to ride a roller coaster.

8 – 12. Word Pairs: Write S if the words are synonyms or A if they are antonyms.

   _____ amusement – boredom   _____ sluggish – lively

   _____ constantly – continually   _____ convince – persuade

   _____ torture – enjoyment   _____ sensible - reasonable

Lesson #17

Renaissance Men

The **Italian Renaissance** is considered a turning point in the history of Western civilization. It marks a time when great thinkers began to look back to the advanced civilizations of Greece and Rome. They reclaimed the long-lost knowledge of those ancient cultures. Art, science, and music flourished throughout the Renaissance. During this time, there were several "Renaissance Men," who not only excelled in a single craft, but seemed capable of doing anything.

Name	Skills	Facts
Leon Battista Alberti (1404 -1472)	architect, painter, sculptor, poet, grammarian, priest, philosopher, writer	wrote several treatises (papers) in which he expressed his ideas about various topics, especially the arts; Alberti was considered an early founder of the Renaissance
Leonardo da Vinci (1452 -1519)	painter, sculptor, architect, scientist, inventor, engineer, writer, musician	considered the first artist of the High Renaissance and one of history's greatest painters; da Vinci made early designs for a helicopter and other inventions; bridges modeled after his designs were built in the early 2000's
Michelangelo Buonarroti (1475 -1564)	sculptor, painter, architect, poet, engineer	considered himself to be a sculptor but is responsible for one of the world's most famous set of paintings: the Sistine Chapel ceiling paintings; known as the creator of one of the world's most famous sculptures, *David*
Galileo Galilei (1564 -1642)	astronomer, physicist, mathematician, philosopher	considered by many to be the father of modern science; one of the first to hypothesize that the laws of nature can be viewed mathematically and that they can be tested; discovered Jupiter's four large moons; supported the belief that the sun (not the Earth) is the center of the universe

1. Where did the Renaissance Men live?

    Greece   Italy   United States   none of these

2. When did the Italian Renaissance occur?

    15th Century   16th Century   17th Century   all of these

3. Why was the Italian Renaissance a turning point in the history of Western civilization?

    A) Many churches got a fresh coat of paint during this time.
    B) It was the first time people read newspapers.
    C) There was a great emphasis on the arts, science, and music.
    D) Important inventions like helicopters and bridges were designed.

4. Which of the Renaissance men were poets?

    _____

5. Before the time of Galileo, what did people believe about our solar system?

    A) People believed that Earth was the center of the universe.
    B) People believed that Jupiter had four moons.
    C) People believed that the Earth revolved around the sun.
    D) People thought that mathematics and science were the same thing.

Write the name of each Renaissance man next to the hint that describes him.

        A) Galileo   B) da Vinci   C) Michelangelo   D) Alberti

6. _____ carved *David* and painted the Sistine Chapel

7. _____ an early founder of the Renaissance

8. _____ created designs for bridges that were later built in the 21st century

9. _____ known as the father of modern science

10 – 12. Match each career name with its description.

    A) an expert in the use of language   _____ philosopher

    B) a designer   _____ grammarian

    C) a truth-seeker   _____ physicist

    D) a scientist who studies matter, energy,   _____ architect
        motion, and force

Lesson #18

Equestrian Therapy, Part I

Some of the activities that other children took for granted were especially challenging for Jamal. He could not always control his limbs, and occasionally, Jamal could not **verbalize** his thoughts. He knew the words, but they didn't always fall off of his tongue in the right way. Jamal had been born with cerebral palsy. Most of the time, he walked with the help of leg braces and crutches, but sometimes he had to use a wheelchair. Playing with the neighborhood children was complicated. Jamal kept pace as best he could, but many kids just did not have the patience for him. It was not uncommon for other kids to call Jamal names or to try to play tricks on him. Jamal understood that some people have trouble accepting those who appear different. He had some really great friends at school. Besides, his two sisters never got tired of spending time with him, and they had always helped him with any difficulties he'd had to face.

Mostly, Jamal was **contented** with his life. He knew that he was intelligent and complete in every way. With the help of his parents and his doctors, he worked at being as physically healthy as possible. Jamal knew his friends and his family appreciated him, and they depended on him, so he didn't feel sorry for himself. All the same, Jamal had a secret: He wondered how it would feel to be just like everybody else. He had never played football or ridden a bike, and those were things that other kids seemed to really enjoy. One day, he mentioned this thought to his grandma, and she said that it would be her greatest joy to help Jamal make his wish come true.

Cerebral is a word that means *having to do with the brain*, and **palsy** is a weakness in the muscles. So, a person with **cerebral palsy** (CP) has trouble controlling his arms and legs because of the way messages travel from the brain to the muscles. For a person who has CP, it is much more difficult to do everyday things like getting dressed, walking, talking, and eating. Kids with this condition can go to school, play with friends, go on vacations with their families, and enjoy many of the same activities as other kids. They like to laugh, make friends, and get good grades. They just need extra time and a little bit of help. It's important to remember that a friend or a classmate with CP wants to fit in as much as anybody else does.

1. Underline the sentence in the selection that tells why Jamal walked with braces or sometimes used a wheel chair.

2. Cerebral palsy is a condition that affects _____.

    A) a person's immune system   C) neither of these
    B) the brain and the muscles   D) both A and B

3. Why do you think the neighborhood kids were sometimes unkind to Jamal?

    A) They were impatient.   C) They were intolerant.
    B) They were insensitive.   D) all of these

4. Jamal wondered what it would be like to _____.

    A) go to school   C) play with neighborhood kids
    B) play on a baseball team   D) be just like everybody else

5. Choose all the character traits which describe Jamal.

    bad-tempered   reckless   appreciative   irrational   contented

6. Underline the part that states an **effect** in this sentence:

    A person with **cerebral palsy** (CP) has trouble controlling his arms and legs because of the way messages travel from the brain to the muscles.

7. From the context clues, you can tell that *verbalize* means _____.

        feelings   speak   walk   language   none of these

8. To whom did Jamal confide his secret?   _____

9. Complete the analogy.   unsure : _____ :: secure : vulnerable

Circle a synonym and underline an antonym for each **bolded** word.

10. **intolerant**   understanding   slow   confused   narrow-minded

11. **challenging**   determined   easy   demanding   nervous

12. **exceptional**   hopeless   calm   commonplace   extraordinary

Lesson #19

Equestrian Therapy, Part II

Soon afterwards, Jamal's grandma picked him up from school and told him she had a grand surprise. He did his best to **extract** the details, but Grandma wouldn't give in. After a long ride into the country, Grandma headed down a lane and pulled the car to a parking spot in front of a huge barn. She beamed at Jamal and informed him that he was about to get his wish. When they entered the barn, a woman wearing tight pants, high black boots, and a funny looking hat welcomed Jamal. She said she was glad to have him as part of their group. Jamal still wasn't quite sure what was going on, but he thanked the lady anyway.

Jamal's grandma pushed his wheel chair onto a ramp that led to an enormous room. A beautiful horse stood quietly, **tethered** to a **horizontal** bar. A man brought Jamal a helmet. Then, he helped Jamal out of his wheel chair and onto the back of the horse. Grandma explained that this was equestrian therapy, and that if Jamal liked what he was about to do, he could come here each week to learn horseback riding.

Immediately, Jamal knew that he would be devoted to horseback riding! He was never afraid, even though the horse was quite large and sometimes snorted loudly. During the weekly lessons, Jamal always rode the same horse, and an instructor was always with him. He learned how to make the horse walk and trot, how to stop, and even how to back up. The instructors told him that the motion of the horse walking could exercise the muscles in Jamal's legs for him. While he was on horseback, Jamal never felt awkward. He felt that he was equal to everybody else and able to do all the things that any other kid on horseback could do. Over time, Jamal's sense of balance improved, his legs got stronger, and most of all, he really had fun!

Equestrian therapy combines horseback riding techniques with physical therapy. The rider learns to control the horse and to move along paths and over obstacles. These **maneuvers** help to strengthen the muscles and to improve the balance, **coordination**, and **endurance** of the rider. The rider also learns to groom the horse, and by caring for it, the rider develops a **therapeutic** bond with the animal. Many people believe that equestrian therapy also helps kids to build **self-esteem**, confidence, and independence.

1. What does the word *equestrian* refer to?   _____

2. What are some of the benefits of equestrian therapy? List as many as you can.

    _____

    _____

3. Underline the part that describes what kind of clothing the instructors wore.

4. How did equestrian therapy allow Jamal to get his wish?

    A) Jamal felt that he was equal to everybody else and able to do all the things that any other kid on horseback could do.
    B) Jamal finally had the pet horse that he had always wanted.
    C) Equestrian therapy cured Jamal of cerebral palsy.
    D) all of the above

Match each word from the selection with the hint that describes it.

5. _____ extract   A) respect for self

6. _____ tethered   B) healing

7. _____ horizontal   C) ability to go on

8. _____ maneuvers   D) remove or pull out

9. _____ coordination   E) tied with leather straps

10. _____ endurance   F) special moves or exercises

11. _____ therapeutic   G) straight and parallel with the ground

12. _____ self-esteem   H) the ability to move smoothly

Lesson #20

Read the following editorial from a middle school newspaper.

Preteens and Privacy: Kids Need their Own Computers, by Jeremy

My parents subscribe to a "parenting magazine" that is chocked full of useful advice for keeping kids like me out of trouble. Mom and Dad leave the magazine lying around, as if tempting me to read up on recommendations for limiting my own privacy. Actually, I did pick up a recent issue. The article I read was entitled, "Avoiding Teen Traps" (as if kids go around trying to **ambush** their parents!). The article recommends that parents resist the urge to put a computer in a kid's bedroom. Instead, the experts strongly suggest that the "family computer" be located in an area of the house where everyone has equal access to it. What the authors are really saying is, "Put the computer out in the open, so you can keep an eye on what those **adolescents** are doing while they're on-line."

I have some objections to this recommendation. First, I use the computer to do school work (mostly), and the open areas of our house are very **chaotic**. The television is on, the phone is ringing, people are talking, and my little brother is crashing his toy trucks into piles of building blocks. That is hardly an ideal environment for concentrating on assignments. My second objection is that it is very difficult to share a computer. I use the internet to do research, and I use word processing programs to complete my assignments. Hence, I would be **monopolizing** the computer for most of the evening. That is not really fair to my younger sister or my parents. Of course, the authors of the magazine article suggest taking turns and using a timer when there are several kids in the household who need access to a computer. This is really not practical, in my opinion. If the timer goes off right in the middle of my research or my writing, I would lose everything and have to start all over again during my next scheduled session.

Parents should just give it up and trust their kids. Anyone in middle school is old enough to have a computer in his bedroom. Technologies are not privileges – they are requirements, especially in today's world. Teachers expect students to have access to technology, and many assignments require the **capacity** to do internet research. What do you think? If you'd like to comment on this editorial, send an e-mail to Jeremy.

1. What is Jeremy trying to communicate in the underlined sentence?

    A) He is mocking the usefulness of parenting magazines.
    B) He is recommending that teens read parenting magazines.
    C) He is noting that parenting magazines are very useful.
    D) He agrees that kids his age do get into a lot of trouble.

2. Jeremy has several reasons why he thinks it is not a good idea to share a computer with his family. Which of these is not one of Jeremy's reasons?

    A) It is too noisy in the common areas of the house.
    B) Computers are very expensive.
    C) Teachers expect students to have access to computers.
    D) There is not enough time to do homework when sharing a computer.

3. What do Jeremy's parents think about the magazine article that Jeremy read?

   A)   They agree with the article.   C)   They have no opinion.

   B)   They disagree with the article.   D)   The information is not given.

4. Why do you think the magazine article recommends that parents resist the urge to put a computer in a kid's bedroom?

   _____

   _____

   _____

Match these words with their meanings. Use context clues.

5. _____ ambush   A) taking over

6. _____ adolescents   B) entrap

7. _____ chaotic   C) ability

8. _____ monopolizing   D) young people

9. _____ capacity   E) hectic, frenzied

Write O if the sentence states an opinion or F if it states a fact.

10. _____ Forty percent of American homes have at least one computer.

11. _____ A chaotic environment is not favorable for doing homework.

12. _____ Most teachers expect students to have a computer at home.

Lesson #21

Letters to the Editor

Dear Jeremy:

    I am writing in response to your editorial about kids needing their own computers. First of all, you wrote that your parents subscribe to a "parenting magazine" that you think they want you to look at, so that you'll stay out of trouble. I just want to say that you are very lucky to have parents who not only care about you, but who will go the extra mile and even get reading material to help them be better parents to you and your siblings. Wow, that's amazing!

    Second, I wish that you had included more information about which other "teen traps" were mentioned in that article, rather than just your own **pet peeve** about having your personal computer. But that's the subject of another letter, I guess.

    I really disagree with what you said. The family computer IS just that — family!! Everybody should be able to use it, just like the family car, the family TV, and the family refrigerator. If the computer is upstairs, it might be inconvenient for someone who needs to look up something important right at that moment. Besides, school is chaotic, yet we manage to get our work done there. So having a work station "out in the open" shouldn't make it that hard to get your homework done. (There are, by the way, fewer people at your house than there are at school). In addition, your parents pay for the computer and other things that come with it. Unless you are responsible for buying the equipment, I suggest that you use it wherever your parents say you should use it. Cooperating with them will go a long way toward having them trust you in the future.

    I have learned that using my computer time wisely (doing assignments ahead of time, for example) makes space for other family members to have their fair share of computer time, and that eliminates most arguments.

Signed,
Rethink Your Options

1.   How does the writer feel about the editorial written by Jeremy?

    A)   agrees with Jeremy   C)   agrees with some of Jeremy's points
    B)   disagrees with Jeremy   D)   no strong opinion either way

2.   What does the writer wish that Jeremy would have included in the article?

_____

_____

3. Why does the writer feel that kids should be able to do homework *out in the open*?

   A) Students work in a chaotic atmosphere at school.
   B) Parents pay for computers and software.
   C) Family members are able to share other things like cars and TV's.
   D) The letter does not say.

4. What is a *pet peeve*? Use the context clues to decide.

   A) a cat, dog, or hamster　　　C) a personal annoyance

   B) a strong opinion　　　　　　D) a fake pet (like a rock)

5. What advice does the writer have for Jeremy?

   A) learn to manage your time　　　C) buy your own computer

   B) do your research at school　　　D) throw away the magazines

6. What is the purpose of editorials and letters-to-the-editor?

   A) to report the facts　　　　　C) to express opinions

   B) to take reader surveys　　　D) to advertise products

Underline the part of each sentence that states a <u>cause</u>.

7. I am able to complete my assignments because I use my computer time wisely.

8. Due to the cost of computer hardware, we can only afford to have one workstation.

Underline the part of each sentence that states an <u>effect</u>.

9. My brother monopolizes the computer, so I do my homework at the library.

10. I have privileges since I follow rules and cooperate with my parents.

Choose the homophone that best completes each sentence.

11. Nicole makes mistakes because she hurries (through / threw) her work.

12. Everyone stood up as soon as the pitcher (through / threw) the ball toward home plate.

Lesson #22

Letters to the Editor

Dear Jeremy:

Your recent article about having a computer in your room really got me thinking. We have our computer in our den at home, and it is a chaotic space. There's lots of activity and noise almost all of the time. I do have a hard time concentrating, sometimes. You bring up a good point about putting time limits on a person's use, so that everyone can have a turn — that's a good idea. We always argue about this at my house, and then someone ends up being really upset. Usually that person is me.

Your thoughts about moving the computer to your room to cut down on chaos, as well as not having to share were important and something to think about. Living in this age of technology means that all of us need access to computers. Homework and internet research are necessities. To be good students, we need all the resources available.

Even beyond this, which you didn't mention, we need to have private use of computers for personal reasons. All of us, or at least most of us, use e-mail to communicate with others. If we don't have computers in our own rooms, then our lives become an open book — just about anyone who walks by can see what we're talking about! I don't think that's a good idea for any relationship. I'm demonstrating that I'm trustworthy when I keep e-mail from friends **confidential**; they don't expect their messages to be read by anyone else. And my parents should know that I'm trying to be a good friend. As long as kids aren't breaking any rules, there is no reason to take away their privacy.

Rather than having computer issues cause a conflict among family members, computers can actually help build up trust when our parents see us using them in adult ways. Thank you for bringing up this very important issue.

Signed,
Keyboarding Keisha

Fact or Opinion? Write F or O.

1. _____ Internet research is a necessity.

2. _____ Computers can help build trust between parents and their children.

3. _____ There is a computer in the living room.

4. _____ Ninety percent of people surveyed communicate via e-mail at least once per week.

5. Underline three **synonyms**. Use a dictionary if you need help.

    talkative   garrulous   unruly   loquacious

6. Underline two **antonyms**. Use a dictionary if you need help.

    industrious   considerate   sincere   lazy

Choose the homophone that correctly completes each sentence.

7. Please put the muffins in a basket as soon as (there / their / they're) ready.

8. All of the children stood freezing in (there / their / they're) wet swimsuits.

9. (There / Their / They're) is a quiet room where you can concentrate.

10 – 12. Read each statement and decide if it supports Jeremy's point of view, or if it is an argument against Jeremy's point of view. Then put the letter of each statement in the appropriate section of the table below.

A) Each person should manage her own time and allow for other family members to use the computer.

B) Kids need privacy when sending and receiving e-mails.

C) Parents are paying for computers, so they should decide where the workstation will be.

D) Having the family computer in someone's bedroom is inconvenient.

E) A common family area can be chaotic, and is not a good work space.

F) A classroom can be chaotic, but kids are still able to do their work.

G) Many family members may need access to a computer; therefore, it should be in a common area.

Supports Jeremy's Point of View	Against Jeremy's Point of View

Lesson #23

Morning Walk

Catching the screen door, so it won't bang shut, I pull on my navy thermal gloves
And search the blue gray sky for any hint of sun.
I walk these mornings seeking big life answers;
I want to know my poetic purpose.
Is mine the path to the right, the path to the left,
Or is it the one in the middle?

Instead, I hear the "tweet-tweet-caw" of the lark sparrow
In elm tree branches overhead.
A patch of crocuses, yellow like butternut squash,
Cuddle up next to some brilliant indigo and periwinkle blooms,
Their yellow centers matching.
From a corner lawn, the flowers scream out, "Look at us!"
My eyes draw next toward pea-green moss
Foaming at the base of a sugar maple.

I duck under a still barren branch, lined with drops of glistening dew,
Listening to a **cacophony** of bird song, car horns, and far-off voices.

1. A simile compares two things using the words *like* or *as*. Underline a **simile** in the poem.

2. What are the two things being compared in the simile?

    _____

A **metaphor** compares two things but does not use the words *like* or *as* in the comparison. In a metaphor, something *is* something else. Here is a metaphor that is used in the poem:

    My eyes draw next toward pea-green moss foaming at the base of a sugar maple.

3. What two things are compared in the metaphor?

    trees and moss   moss and foam

    the color of peas and moss   eyes and a drawing

4. What is the author's purpose for taking morning walks?

    A) The author is bird-watching.
    B) The author hopes to pick a bouquet of spring flowers.
    C) The author is seeking big life answers.
    D) The author wants to get out into the sun.

5. From the way it is used in the poem, you can tell that **cacophony** means what?

    A) a type of soft symphonic music
    B) a mixture of sounds that do not necessarily go together
    C) a choir singing in harmony

6. **Personification** means giving human characteristics to non-human things. Which of the following are examples of personification? Put a check next to any that are.

    _____ Crocuses cuddle up next to some brilliant indigo and periwinkle blooms.

    _____ I hear the "tweet-tweet-caw" of the lark sparrow in elm tree branches.

    _____ From the corner lawn, the flowers scream out, "Look at us!"

    _____ I duck under a still barren branch, lined with drops of glistening dew.

7. Complete the analogy.   bud : flower :: tadpole : _____

List three **synonyms** for each character trait listed below. (See the Help Pages for assistance.)

8. grouchy _____

9. greedy _____

Choose the homophone that correctly completes each sentence.

10. Follow this (rowed / road / rode) until you see a sign for the highway.

11. After the motor quit, we (rowed / road / rode) all the way to the dock.

12. Phyllis (rowed / road / rode) in the convertible with her brother.

Lesson #24

In each description, find one word that is used incorrectly. Circle the incorrect word. Then write an **antonym** that will make the writing accurate. An example has been done for you.

A pilot needs to pay attention to fuel gauges, weather conditions, speed, altitude, and more all at once. Piloting an airplane is rigorous and can be very (relaxing.)

replacement word: _____ stressful _____

1. A microscope is a laboratory tool that is used to magnify objects. Microscopes are helpful for seeing objects that are too large to view with the eyes alone.

   replacement word: _____

2. In 1849, it was unheard of for a woman to go to college. But that year, Elizabeth Blackwell became the first woman to earn her degree as a medical doctor. After receiving acceptance from every leading medical school, she was finally admitted to a medical school in Geneva, New York.

   replacement word: _____

3. Scavengers help to clean up the environment by eating the bodies of dead animals. Decomposers break down what is left before scavengers have finished eating. Scavengers and decomposers have important roles in the food chain.

   replacement word: _____

4. Orville and Wilbur Wright built the world's very first airplane, and on December 17, 1903, the Wright brothers completed their "first flight." Their invention made long-distance travel impossible for thousands of people all over the world.

   replacement word: _____

5. Thomas Edison is best known for conceiving the first long-lasting light bulb, although his favorite invention was the phonograph. As one of the greatest inventors of all time, Edison had fewer inventions than any other inventor.

   replacement word: _____

6. Americans depend upon fossil fuels to supply the energy they need to heat their homes, but there are serious disadvantages to using fossil fuels. Because of this, conservationists are looking for ways to destroy natural resources and develop more renewable energy resources.

    replacement word: _____

Read this description from a public park brochure. Then complete the items that follow.

Soothing Sounds and Sugar Maples

   Pass the mile marker for Neptune, then Saturn, in Euclid Creek Park. Make a right, turn in, and park your car. You'll hear it before you see it. Its rushing sounds play off the trunks of the trees, and the echoes of its constant flow volley between the pin oak and sugar maple leaves. As you step between bulging roots and protruding rocks descending the embankment of the creek, you'll be amazed by the solid blue stone rising up like a canyon wall. Soothing sounds are created by water surging over the flat shale stones. Find a dry boulder and sit for awhile. If you let it inside you, it'll whisper startling truths:

   "It's all changing. Life has times of gentle rocking. Life wears you down and then brings you surprises: a blue dragonfly riding a red maple leaf raft for free. Find the places of stillness; the noises are an orchestra performance."

7. The description says, "You'll hear it before you see it." What is the thing you will hear?

    _____

Read each of the phrases taken from the above selection and decide which literary device is used in each. Write **S** for simile, **P** for personification, or **M** for metaphor.

8. _____ it'll whisper startling truths

9. _____ the noises are an orchestra performance

10. _____ Life wears you down and then brings you surprises

11. _____ solid blue stone rising up like a canyon wall

12. _____ a blue dragonfly riding a red maple leaf raft for free

Lesson #25

The Day the Nurse Came

I'll never forget the day after my seventh birthday. On that day, the traveling school nurse came to my second grade class with a **stethoscope** around her neck and a portable doctor's office scale. It was the kind of scale with a sliding thin metal bar that she would lay on top of your head to measure how tall you were. Then she'd move the wrought iron weight along the horizontal bar to the place where it stayed perfectly balanced. This point marked how much you weighed. My father had promised me that Grandad would give me a toy doctor's kit if I gained enough weight to reach 75 pounds. I don't remember how tall I was on that day, but I do remember the nurse's exact words:

"Seventy-six and one fourth pounds, Miss Mary," she said.

Of course I was close to exploding with excitement, but I was not of a **temperament** to **disclose** my **glee** to anyone else. In Mrs. Pearson's class, I had no **chums** close enough to be worthy of receiving such **particulars**. Anyway, I actually thought I was too fat, so body weight was a lunchroom topic I would avoid at any cost. I had to simply **bask** in the warmth of my secret for the rest of that **interminable** day. At last, the school day ended and I got off the school bus, galloped along the gravel driveway, and burst into the kitchen with my news:

"Mom, call Granddad! Tell him I weigh seventy-six and one fourth pounds! Tell him now!"

Mom shared in my delight, basking quietly in her own secret – a deep sense of relief. Her little girl was healthy! During these scary times of the worsening polio **epidemic**, gaining weight was a sure sign of safe passage.

In the early part of the twentieth century, many children were left crippled or even died from a disease called polio. No one knew where the virus came from. There was no vaccine against polio and no cure for the ailment.

---

1. Why did Mary's father promise her a toy doctor's kit?

    A) It was a secret.
    B) Mary's parents hoped she would become a doctor.
    C) Mary wanted to be a nurse.
    D) He was enticing Mary to eat more and gain weight.

2. Underline three **synonyms**.

       glee   chums   bask   pals   friends

3.　Mary's mom had a secret of her own.　She believed that *gaining weight was a sure sign of safe passage*.　What is another way of saying this?

A)　Eating well helps children to travel safely.
B)　By second grade, a child should weigh at least 75 pounds.
C)　Mary's ability to gain weight meant that she wouldn't get polio.
D)　Certain foods will prevent the spread of the polio virus.

4.　Mary says that she *was not of a temperament to disclose her glee*.　What is another way of saying this?

A)　Mary had an introverted personality, so she kept things to herself.
B)　Mary didn't have any friends at school.
C)　Mary didn't want anyone to hear her laughing.
D)　Mary was afraid of getting into trouble for talking in class.

Use context clues to help you match each word with its meaning.

5.　_____ particulars　　　A) never-ending

6.　_____ temperament　　　B) reveal

7.　_____ epidemic　　　C) details

8.　_____ interminable　　　D) personality

9.　_____ disclose　　　E) outbreak

Write *C* if the underlined part states a cause or *E* if it states an effect.

10.　_____　Parents were terrified of the disease since <u>no one knew what caused polio and there was no cure</u>.

11.　_____　As a result of the vaccine developed by Dr. Jonas Salk, <u>the polio epidemic ended after 1955</u>.

12.　_____　I actually thought I was too fat, so <u>body weight was a lunchroom topic I would avoid at any cost</u>.

Lesson #26

My Friend, Margaret: A Memoir

It's spring 1946. I can call her Margaret, and I like that. Most grown-ups have to be called "Miss" or "Misses." She'd be Miss Gilfillan, according to Mom. John and Alexander are her brothers, and they all live on the farm across from us. The Gilfillans feed their cows, drive a tractor, cut hay, shear sheep, and do stuff like that. Some days the two brothers work downtown, like my Dad. Only, they don't ride the bus. They drive their big black car. But Margaret is always home. Mom lets me go over to visit extra early today.

"Hi Margaret," I shout, spotting her waiting for me at the top of the lane.

"Hi Mary," she replies with her warm quiet voice. Her expression is so beautiful. It shines like the face of the moon.

"Are we gathering eggs, today?" I ask in my please-make-this-be-the-day voice. She's holding the two brown baskets with wads of cotton covering the bottoms.

"Yes, and fresh milk from the spring house," she answers. I'm **ecstatic** to be hunting for fresh warm eggs in the chicken coop. Margaret taught me how to **converse** with the hens, so they won't be angry about losing their eggs; we make clucking sounds like they do.

We leave the eggs at the back door and head for the spring house down by the creek. We pick up a pale of fresh milk, still cooling in the water trough from early morning when the brothers milked the cows. I never seem to get here on time for that, but Margaret's promised to show me how to do the milking. I love Margaret. She always keeps promises.

On the days when we gather eggs and bring in the milk, we always get to make bread and churn butter in the big yellow kitchen. While the bread bakes and that yummy smell floats through the house hanging right around my nostrils, I play with the pipe cleaners. Margaret showed me how to make people by bending and twisting them. Today I decide to make a model of myself. I use white for my body and a black one wound around the circle-face for my hair. Margaret smiles with delight when I give it to her.

"Why, thank you. You know, I think I'll keep this little Mary forever, right here." She tucks one of the little feet into the frame of the mirror by the hallway.

It's fall 1999. Visiting my hometown for Thanksgiving at my brother's, I decide to drive out to the farm for one of my rare visits with Margaret. I've called ahead to announce my arrival. As she greets me and I walk through the back door, I have the sensation of going back in time. Margaret is still smiling. She's nearly 100 years old. Alexander and John have both passed on. Margaret seems content to remain in the old farmhouse with her full-time caretaker. I'm following her through the kitchen toward the front parlor. As we cross into the hallway, I glance to my right. What do I see, but little pipe cleaner Mary, still attached to the same corner of the same mirror. I love my friend Margaret. She always keeps her promises.

1. The narrator is the person telling the story. Circle the name of the narrator in the selection.

2. Underline a **simile** in the third paragraph.

3. What are the two things being compared in the simile?

_____   _____

4. **Memoir** comes from a Latin word, meaning *memory*. A memoir is a story of someone's personal experiences. The excerpt recounts two memories. When did the events take place?

_____

5. What is unusual about the friendship described in the first part of the story?
    A)   The friends live very far away from each other.
    B)   One friend is an adult and the other is a child.
    C)   The friends gather eggs and bake bread together.
    D)   The friends communicate by making clucking sounds.

Below are lists of **synonyms**. Cross out the words that don't belong.

6.   disappointed   ecstatic   overjoyed   thrilled   delighted

7.   speak   communicate   converse   talk   predict

8. Why was it surprising that the pipe cleaner doll was attached to the hall mirror at the end of the story?

_____

Fact or Opinion? Write **F** or **O**.

9.   _____ Nitrogen gas makes up over 75% of the air around us; over 20% is oxygen.

10. _____ It is difficult to breathe in a room that contains cigarette smoke.

11. _____ Physics is a fascinating branch of science because it covers many topics.

12. _____ Physics is defined as the science of energy and matter.

Lesson #27

Jimmy Sloane

I don't even know what school Jimmy Sloane goes to. He doesn't go to mine. Or if he does, I never see him there. But Jimmy is my friend. Margaret introduced us. His parents rent the small wooden farmhouse that is across from the big brick farmhouse where Margaret lives. Jimmy's my age, I'm sure of that. He's skinny and wears his hair real short in a brush cut. Maybe it's called a "brush cut" because the short hairs stand up, and when you rub your hand over the top of his head, it feels like a soft hairbrush. He has freckles and big front teeth. My mother says he has buck teeth. What's that? It must be something bad, because Mom told me not to say that to Jimmy.

One Saturday, Jimmy comes over to my house to play. This is the first time, since we usually play over at the farm. Before we met, Jimmy told Margaret that he wasn't sure whether he wanted to play with a girl. Margaret told Mom, and she told me. Then I guess Margaret told him not to worry, that I could do anything a boy could do – especially playing outdoors. So, on this first visit, I show Jimmy my clubhouse. My clubhouse is really the chicken coop, but I took it over last week after Daddy killed that last rooster. He and Mom have decided there'll be no more chickens – too much work, protecting them from foxes, for one thing. Then there's all that yucky stuff Mom has to do to get them from the chicken coop to the table, like plucking all the feathers and cleaning out the insides. I admit I like to sneak upstairs and look out the window when Daddy chops off their heads. They run around like crazy with no heads before they drop over. Mom refuses to watch. I guess it makes her kind of sick.

Anyway, Jimmy and I play in my clubhouse and pretend we're chasing bad guys. I show him the best climbing trees in the apple orchard and my hideout in the bushes down by the creek. We catch crayfish and pretend we're cooking them for our supper. Meanwhile, we've already caught the bad guys. They're locked up in the clubhouse. The next time I see Margaret, she tells me Jimmy doesn't mind playing with girls anymore. I really don't get it.

1. The narrator is the person telling the story. About how old is the narrator of this story?

    8 years old   unknown   20 years old   65 years old

2. Is the narrator male or female?   _____

3.   According to the narrator, how old is Jimmy Sloane?

    A)   the same age as the narrator   C)   about 9 years old

    B)   high school-aged   D)   Jimmy is an adult.

4.   Underline the sentence that tells how the narrator met Jimmy Sloane.

5.   Who is locked up in the clubhouse?

   chickens   other children   imaginary bad guys   none of these

6.   According to the narrator, why have Mom and Dad decided there will be no more chickens?

    A)   It's too much trouble to keep chickens.
    B)   The chicken coop has been converted to a clubhouse.
    C)   Chickens are very expensive to keep.
    D)   Nobody will eat the eggs.

Underline the part that states a <u>cause</u>.

7.   Jimmy doesn't play with girls because he thinks girls are not fun.

8.   It's not polite to say someone has buck teeth, so Mom says, "Don't say that to Jimmy."

Underline the part that states an <u>effect</u>.

9.   The top of his head feels like a soft hairbrush; that's why it's called a "brush cut."

10.   I know Jimmy doesn't go to my school because I never see him there.

Choose the homophone that correctly completes each sentence.

11.   I show Jimmy my clubhouse because (its / it's) the first time he has come over to play.

12.   A chicken will continue running around even without (its / it's) head.

Lesson #28

Vocabulary Review

Complete the crossword puzzle on the next page. Use bolded words from previous lessons.

Across

3. a turning point in the history of Western civilization (Lesson #17)
5. catch, grab, grasp (Lesson #13)
10. special moves or exercises (Lesson #19)
11. compares two things using the words *like* or *as* (Lesson #23)
12. hectic, frenzied (Lesson #20)
13. collection of samples of a person's best work (Lesson #15)
15. polished (Lesson #14)
16. having to do with horseback riding (Lesson #19)
17. miniature (Lesson #12)
18. personality (Lesson #25)
19. overjoyed (Lesson #26)

Down

1. compares two things by saying something is something else (Lesson #23)
2. giving human characteristics to non-human things (Lesson #23)
4. the enemy or "bad guy" in a story (Lesson #12)
6. a story of someone's personal experiences (Lesson #26)
7. entrap, lay in wait (Lesson #20)
8. having to do with the brain (Lesson #18)
9. the ability to go on (Lesson #19)
12. private, secret (Lesson #22)
14. sociable, companionable (Lesson #13)

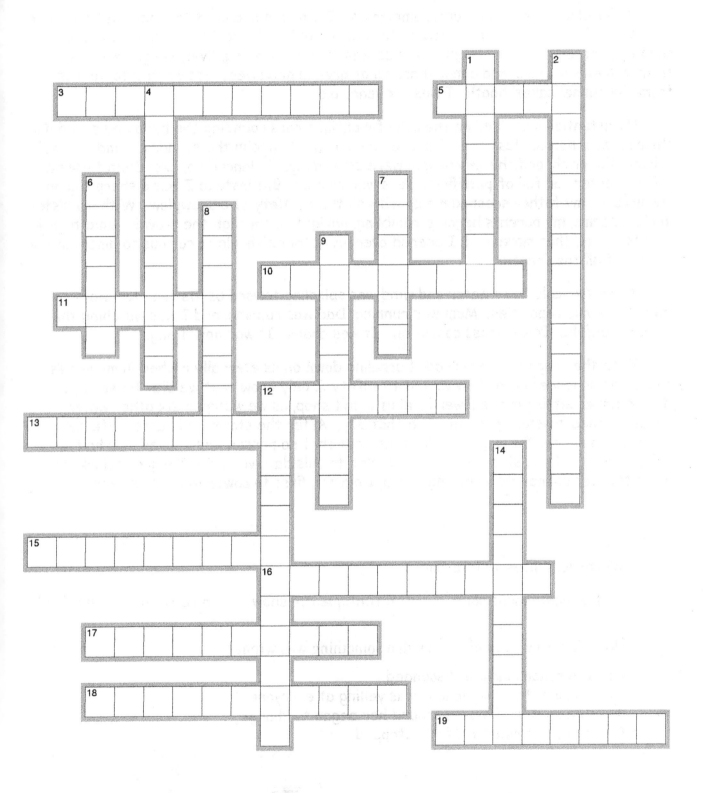

Lesson #29

A Narrow Escape

Under clear skies, on a warm summer day, I stood in line next to Mom and Dad – and my sister, of course. We were waiting to ride the old-fashioned cars, and everything seemed perfectly normal. People were screaming and laughing; lively songs **resonated** from unseen speakers, and a mixed aroma of grease and sweetness wafted toward us from the funnel cakes' booth. I was six years old.

My attention was fixed on the colorful antique cars rounding the bend and sounding their musical horns. Just then, I sensed an abrupt change in the sounds around us: the volume, the pitch, and the *way* people were screaming. I glanced up, expecting to see a roller coaster car full of **petrified** riders whizzing by. But instead I felt a sharp tug on my arms, as my father scooped me up with all the **subtlety** of a snowplow. With my sister in Mom's arms, my parents began scrambling, navigating through the crowd. Amid frantic shouts and all that movement, I peered over my father's shoulder, curious to discover the source of all the frenzy.

A colossal column of water and wind was spiraling toward us, its roar forewarning its **cataclysmic** capacities. Mom was running, Dad was running, and I was watching the disaster unfold. It was mass confusion. It was chaos. It was horrifying.

With the image of the tornado barreling down on us **eternally etched** in my mind's eye, I can no longer recall how we got to safety; I only know that we did. However, I do remember sitting in the lower level of a gift shop, as we watched six other water spouts-turned-twisters pass through that day. After the storm had passed, life suddenly emerged to survey the damage. We found out that no person was injured, nor had any ride, eatery, or little shop been harmed. Yet, to this day, when the sky grows dark, or when thunder sounds its menacing alarm, I am the first to **cower** in the basement.

1. Where does the story take place?

    at an amusement park   at an antique car show   on a farm   in a field

2. How did the narrator first know that something was wrong?
    A) a tornado alarm was sounded
    B) a man with a megaphone was yelling at everyone
    C) the sounds of voices around her began to change
    D) all of the rides suddenly stopped

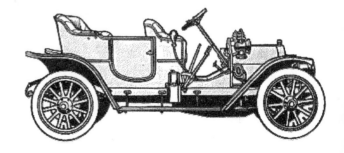

3.   The narrator says, "My father scooped me up with all the subtlety of a snowplow."
     What is another way of saying this?

     A)   My father grabbed me as fast as he could, not taking the time to be gentle.
     B)   My father pushed me aside like a pile of snow on a cold winter's day.
     C)   My father tenderly lifted me; I felt like I was floating in zero gravity.
     D)   My father was too busy moving the snow to worry about me.

4.   The narrator says that the tornado made a sound that was "forewarning its cataclysmic
     capacities." What are cataclysmic capacities?

     extremely loud noises   destructive powers

     exciting entertainment   none of these

5.   How did the narrator and her family find a place that was safe from the storm?

     A) a rescue squad helped them   C) they were evacuated by bus
     B) they were taken away by helicopter D) the narrator does not remember

6.   Underline the phrase that lets the reader know that the narrator will never forget what she
     saw that day.

Use context clues to match each word with its meaning.

7.   _____ resonated   A) forever

8.   _____ petrified   B) imprinted

9.   _____ subtlety   C) resounded, echoed

10. _____ cower   D) terrified

11. _____ etched   E) cringe, shy away

12. _____ eternally   F) delicacy

Lesson #30

Tornadoes

   Like other types of severe weather, tornadoes can be both dangerous and destructive. A tornado may also be known as a twister, a whirlwind, or a cyclone. It is a rotating column of air that forms at the bottom of a storm cloud and stretches down to touch the Earth. Storms develop in the presence of warm, moist air, and this warm moist air coming from one direction meets up with cool dry air coming from another direction. Warm air rises, and strong winds cause the warm rising air to spin. As the funnel cloud spins, more air rushes in to replace the rising air. The spinning air pulls objects into the tornado – this is the perilous and destructive part. Everything from dirt and trees to pieces of houses and even cars can be sucked off the ground and sent crashing into whatever is in the path of a tornado. Twisters can travel at speeds of up to 300 miles per hour, and they reach an average of 500 feet across, although some can be even a mile wide. A strong tornado can travel for several miles before it eventually dies down.

   These violent storms are especially likely to occur in an area known as "Tornado Alley," a region in the central plains that includes parts of North Dakota, South Dakota, Nebraska, Kansas, Oklahoma, and Texas. *But tornadoes can and do occur anywhere.* That is why it's very important to be educated and prepared for severe weather. There are two important phrases used by the National Weather Service to alert people about the possibility of a twister: tornado watch and tornado warning. A **tornado watch** means that tornadoes are possible under the current weather conditions. During a tornado watch, it is important to stay close to a television or radio, so you can receive up-to-the-minute news about any developing twister. A **tornado warning** means that a tornado has been sighted nearby. When there is a tornado warning, you should take shelter immediately. The best place to take cover is in a basement; the next best place is a hallway or an inside room that has no windows. If you are at school, it is likely that there is a plan for protecting everyone. You should listen carefully and follow directions.

   After a tornado, there may be downed power lines, broken glass, and many other hazardous situations. There may even be injured people. Never touch electrical lines, and stay away from loosely hanging tree limbs or other precarious objects. If someone is hurt, get help as soon as possible.

1. Give three other names for a tornado.

   _____   _____   _____

2. True or False?

   _____ Tornadoes occur in all parts of the United States.

3.   What is the difference between a tornado watch and a tornado warning?

   A)   There is no difference.
   B)   A tornado warning is more serious than a tornado watch.
   C)   A warning means a tornado may develop; a watch means a tornado has already
        been seen.
   D)   A watch is announced on the TV or radio; a tornado warning comes from the
        National Weather Service.

Cross out the word that is NOT a synonym of all the others.

4.   perilous   dangerous   protected   hazardous   treacherous

5.   precarious   unstable   insecure   unsteady   balanced

Underline the part that states a <u>cause</u>.

6.   Warm moist air meets cool dry air; as a result, the rising warm air spins.

7.   Students know what to do during a tornado since schools have periodic tornado
     drills.

Underline the part that states an <u>effect</u>.

8.   A tornado can be quite perilous because the spinning air sends objects crashing
     into anything in its path.

9.   Today, fewer people are injured and killed during tornadoes due to the advanced
     warning systems put into place by the National Weather Service.

Write F if the sentence states a fact or O if it states an opinion.

10.   _____   Tornado alley is not a very safe place to live.

11.   _____   This town has an underground shelter where people can go for
                 protection during severe weather.

12.   _____   All public schools, hospitals, and office buildings should have
                 tornado safety plans.

Level 6

Reading Comprehension

Help Pages

Help Pages

Analogy

An **analogy** is a way of comparing things.

Here is an example: mayor : city :: governor : state

This means,

"Mayor is to city as governor is to state."

To solve an analogy, you need to figure out what the relationship is between the two words.

A *mayor* is <u>the leader of</u> a *city*. A *governor* is <u>the leader of</u> a *state*.

Here is another example: lamb : sheep :: calf : _____

horse   piglet   cow   kitten

What is the relationship?   A lamb is <u>a baby</u> sheep.

The missing word must be *cow* because a *calf* is <u>a baby</u> *cow*.

In an **analogy**, the words may be compared in many ways.

The words may be synonyms.

Example: happy : joyful :: tall : high

Happy and *joyful* are <u>synonyms</u>. *Tall* and *high* are <u>synonyms,</u> too.

The words may be antonyms.

Example: thin : fat :: rich : poor

Thin is the <u>opposite</u> of *fat*. *Rich* is the <u>opposite</u> of *poor*.

One word may describe the other.

Example: bright : sunshine :: prickly : porcupine

Sunshine is *bright*. A *porcupine* is *prickly*.

One word may name a part of the other.

Example: wheels : bicycle :: legs : table

A *bicycle* has *wheels*. A *table* has *legs*.

One word may be in the category or group of the other.

Example: rabbit : mammal :: orange : fruit

A *rabbit* is a type of *mammal*. An *orange* is a type of *fruit*.

Help Pages

Context Clues

You can use **context clues** to figure out the meaning of a word. Context clues are the words that come before or after the unknown word.

Sometimes the author will give the definition of the new word by using **synonyms**.

> Example 1: The farmers get fair **remuneration** or
> payment for the goods they provide.

The context clues let you know that *remuneration* must mean *payment*.

> Example 2: Margo's biggest **gaffe** was that she called the
> teacher by her first name. That was a mistake!

You can tell that *gaffe* means *mistake*. The next sentence says exactly that. Also, you probably know that calling a teacher by her first name would be a mistake.

Sometimes the author will hint about the meaning of the word by using **antonyms**.

> Example 1: Claire was actually **garrulous** this morning.
> Usually she barely speaks.

The context clues let you know that *garrulous* must mean the opposite of *barely speaks*. So, *garrulous* must mean *talkative*.

> Example 2: When the teacher was gone during recess, the
> kindergarten room was **chaotic**! I longed for my
> own peaceful, quiet classroom.

You can tell that *chaotic* means the opposite of *peaceful and quiet*. Also, you can imagine recess in a room full of five-year-olds without their teacher.

If you cannot figure out the meaning of a word, it's a good idea to first decide what part of speech the word is.

> Example: Dr. Foster had photos of beautiful **tetras** in his office.

Which of these tells the meaning of *tetras*? acrobats   cooking   fish   jumps
This sentence doesn't tell you what *tetras* are, but you can tell that *tetra* is a *plural noun*. So it is probably not *cooking* or *jumps*.

> Read the next part: Tetras are so brightly colored! Imagine
> seeing them swimming in large schools in
> the clear rivers of South America.

Which of these tells the meaning of *tetras*? acrobats   ~~cooking~~   fish   ~~jumps~~
The context clues – *swimming in large schools in the clear rivers of South America* – tell you that *tetras* must be a *type of colorful fish*.

Help Pages

Fact or Opinion

A **fact** can be proven. An **opinion** tells what someone thinks or believes. Here are some examples.

> Example: There is a rock climbing wall at the recreation center.

This is a fact because you see the wall at the recreation center. It is definitely there.

> Example: Rock climbing is fun, but it can also be dangerous.

This is an opinion because *fun* and *dangerous* mean different things to different people.

Look for **clue words** like can, should, always, never, may and phrases like I think, I believe, and I feel. **These words usually signal an opinion.**

Sometimes part of a sentence is factual and another part states an opinion.

> Example: The rules won't allow anyone under the age of 12 to climb the rock wall, and that isn't fair.

The first part of the sentence can be proven – just check the rock-climbing rules. The second part of the sentence is an opinion because the meaning of *fair* differs from person to person.

Here is another example:

The Rock 'n Roll Gym has both indoor and outdoor climbing walls, (Fact) so it is a much better place to climb. (Opinion)

Cause and Effect

An **effect** tells <u>what</u> happened. The **cause** tells <u>why</u> it happened.

> Example: Cause ➡ There was a blizzard overnight,
> Effect ➡ and the roads are closed today.

Ask yourself, "What happened?" The roads are closed. (Effect)

Ask yourself, "Why did it happen?" There was a blizzard overnight. (Cause)

A cause may have more than one effect.

> Example: Cause ➡ There was a blizzard overnight,
> Effects ➡ so the roads are closed today and
> snow plows have to work overtime.

Help Pages

Cause and Effect (continued)

An effect may be the cause of something else.

> Example: Cause ➡ The roads are closed today;
> Effect ➡ therefore school is cancelled.
>
> Cause ➡ Since school is cancelled,
> Effect ➡ we are taking our sleds to the park.

blizzard ➡ roads closed ➡ schools cancelled ➡ sled rides in the park

Sometimes special clue words and phrases can signal a cause or effect.

as a result of	consequently	hence	so	thus
because	due to	since	therefore	

Remember, the <u>order</u> of cause and effect statements can change. Either can come first in a sentence.

> Example: Cause ➡ The oven got too hot,
> Effect ➡ so the cookies burned.
>
> Effect ➡ The cookies burned
> Cause ➡ because the oven got too hot.

Character Traits

Character traits are features that describe a story character. You can tell a little about a character by the way he acts, the things he says, and even the thoughts he has. The author will always give you clues that tell about the traits of the main character.

> Example: "I hope Mom doesn't give those kids any of our new crayons," thought Cindy. Cindy would never share her toys with the other kids. She even hid her basket of candy whenever her cousins came to her house to play.

Which character trait describes Cindy?   generous   friendly   selfish

Cindy is *selfish*. Other words that describe this character trait are *stingy, self-centered,* and *grudging*.

Help Pages

Character Traits (continued)

Here is a list of character traits. All of the words are adjectives that describe a person or a character. The words are grouped together by similar meaning.

active	**adventurous**	**affectionate**	**ambitious**
energetic	bold	loving	motivated
lively	daring	warm	striving
dynamic	enterprising	friendly	pushy
busy		kind	

angry	**annoying**	**babyish**	**bewildered**
disgruntled	irritating	immature	confused
irritated	bothersome	childish	puzzled
cranky	insufferable	infantile	befuddled
cross			

bossy	**brave**	**careful**	**charming**
dominant	courageous	cautious	delightful
interfering	gutsy	alert	pleasant
controlling	fearless	watchful	agreeable
		attentive	

clever	**conceited**	**cowardly**	**crafty**
bright	self-important	gutless	cunning
witty	vain	spineless	sneaky
sharp	smug	weak	sly
	arrogant		devious

curious	**deceitful**	**determined**	**diligent**
inquisitive	devious	strong-minded	hard-working
probing	dishonest	unwavering	thorough
questioning	untrustworthy	firm	meticulous
			industrious

eager	**efficient**	**foolish**	**friendly**
enthusiastic	well-organized	unwise	welcoming
wholehearted	competent	silly	gracious
passionate	capable	thoughtless	affable
willing	resourceful	irrational	jovial
			cordial

Help Pages

Character Traits (continued)

funny comical humorous amusing	**generous** giving big-hearted charitable	**gentle** calm mild tender kind-hearted	**greedy** insatiable gluttonous ravenous
grouchy bad-tempered irritable grumpy	**gullible** innocent trusting susceptible naïve	**happy** jovial cheerful jolly good-humored	**hateful** cold-hearted unfeeling cruel
helpful cooperative supportive encouraging	**honest** fair truthful straightforward	**hospitable** open warm friendly welcoming	**humble** modest unassuming
imaginative creative inventive artistic	**impulsive** reckless hasty uncontrolled	**independent** self-sufficient self-reliant	**jealous** envious resentful spiteful
kind compassionate loving empathetic	**lazy** lackadaisical careless half-hearted	**loyal** faithful trustworthy dependable reliable	**malicious** wicked mean nasty cruel
mischievous naughty disobedient wayward	**nervous** edgy tense jumpy fretful anxious	**nosy** meddlesome snooping prying	**obedient** dutiful respectful reverent
opinionated intolerant prejudiced narrow-minded	**optimistic** hopeful positive buoyant upbeat	**pessimistic** hopeless negative glum gloomy	**proud** confident self-assured secure

Help Pages

Character Traits (continued)

quarrelsome	**rebellious**	**responsible**	**rude**
difficult	defiant	dependable	impolite
unreasonable	insolent	conscientious	disrespectful
cantankerous	unruly	trustworthy	vulgar
selfish	**shrewd**	**shy**	**sincere**
stingy	sharp	timid	genuine
self-centered	insightful	bashful	truthful
grudging	wise	introverted	earnest
	clever		
slovenly	**sociable**	**stubborn**	**studious**
sloppy	easy-going	obstinate	academic
disheveled	amiable	headstrong	industrious
untidy	outgoing	inflexible	scholarly
messy			
talkative	**thankful**	**thoughtful**	**thrifty**
chatty	grateful	considerate	frugal
garrulous	appreciative	caring	prudent
loquacious		attentive	economical
wordy			penny-wise
unhappy			
gloomy			
sorrowful			
sad			
dejected			

Homophones

Homophones sound the same, but they have **different meanings and different spellings.** Each homophone in this section is used in a sentence that shows its meaning.

Acts	Barry **acts** tough, but he is really very friendly.
Ax	Use a sharp **ax** to chop the branches off that tree.
Ad	Jay put an **ad** in the newspaper to sell her bike.
Add	**Add** these numbers and write the sum below.
Allowed	No one is **allowed** in the locker room during the game.
Aloud	Read the poem **aloud**, so you can hear the rhyming words.

Help Pages

Homophones (continued)

Ant	Let's move our picnic basket away from the **ant** hill.
Aunt	My dad's sister is my **aunt** (also pronounced änt, as in fäther).
Ate	The Lindens **ate** stew with fresh bread for dinner.
Eight	The number **eight** comes after the number seven.
Bare	Once the autumn leaves have fallen, the tree branches are **bare**.
Bear	A polar **bear** prefers cold weather.
Base	The batter hit a double and easily made it to second **base**.
Bass	The **bass** drum makes a deep, low sound.
Be	My parents warned us to **be** careful during trick-or-treating.
Bee	The **bee** makes honey, a great breakfast food for anyone!
Beat	Be sure to **beat** the eggs and sugar until they are well blended.
Beet	Nila pulled a fully grown **beet** from the vegetable garden.
Bite	Wearing braces on your teeth will improve your **bite**.
Byte	In computer talk, **byte** is short for "binary term."
Blew	Jenna **blew** out seven candles on her birthday cake.
Blue	Mark's favorite color is **blue**.
Board	Would you like a skate **board** or a snow board?
Bored	Adam was **bored** with TV; he wanted to play outside.
Bread	Aunt Felicia makes sweet **bread** with raisins and walnuts.
Bred	The horses were **bred** to be strong and to run very fast.
Brake	The car stops easily, but the **brake** light is on.
Break	If you drop the china doll, it will **break**.
Buy	If we have time to go to the market, I will **buy** some tomatoes.
By	It will be time to eat **by** the time we get home.
Bye	The baby waves when you say, "**bye**-bye."
Cell	If you need to reach me, dial my **cell** phone number.
Sell	This year we will **sell** magazines as a fund-raiser.
Cheap	We buy the **cheap** paper; it works as well as the expensive kind.
Cheep	In the morning, we can hear the "**cheep**, cheep" of hungry chicks.
Close	It's starting to rain, so **close** all the windows.
Clothes	Pick up your **clothes** and put them in the laundry basket.
Grate	Dad's job is to **grate** the cheese for the spaghetti.
Great	This is a **great** day for sledding in the park.
Groan	The angry giant let out a loud **groan** when he saw Jack.
Grown	Now that the trees are fully **grown**, they produce fruit.

Help Pages

Homophones (continued)	
Hair Hare	Lucy likes to comb the doll's **hair** with my hairbrush. A rabbit and a **hare** are similar except for the size of their ears.
Hear Here	The music was so loud, I couldn't **hear** what you were saying. My uncle lives in Germany, but my grandparents live **here**.
Heard Herd	No one **heard** the doorbell ringing. A **herd** of goats was grazing on the hillside.
Hoarse Horse	Judy sounds a little **hoarse**; I think she has a sore throat. Peter keeps a **horse** and some other animals in the barn.
Hole Whole	Kevin dug a **hole** in the ground and filled it with water. You'd better bring two pies; Andy can eat a **whole** pie by himself!
Hour Our	It takes an **hour** to walk from my house to the city pool. We packed our lunches and loaded up **our** backpacks.
Its It's	The kitten is too young to be taken away from **its** mother. We won't have time to go to the shop because **it's** getting late. (it is)
Know No	I **know** the names of all the state capitols. There is **no** milk in the refrigerator.
One Won	The recipe calls for **one** and three-fourths cups of flour. Our team **won** the game by only a few points.
Pail Pale	Sam filled a **pail** with soapy water and began to soap up the car. Walter liked soft, light colors; he used a **pale** yellow on the walls.
Pair Pear	Kim pulled on a **pair** of hip boots and waded into the icy water. The **pear** tree was full of ripe green fruit.
Pray Prey	At Hanukkah, Zoe goes to temple to **pray** and to read scripture. The predator – a hungry lion – stalked its **prey** for hours.
Principal Principle	Remember, the **principal** is your "pal" at school. A **principle** is a basic truth or law, like the principle of relativity.
Read Red	We **read** chapter three, and then we answered the questions. We saw the gates and **red** lights, so we knew a train was coming.
Right Write	I am **right**-handed even though my father is left-handed. Sophie will **write** the play, and the rest of us will design scenery.
Road Rode Rowed	The new apartment complex was built on Willow **Road**. Nora and Tony **rode** the ponies along the dirt trail. We **rowed** for hours and finally set the canoe ashore at sundown.

Help Pages

Homophones (continued)

Role Roll	Nicky will play the **role** of Peter Pan in the school play. The children liked to **roll** down the hill, laughing all the way.
Sail Sale	The ship, filled with passengers, finally set **sail** that morning. Mom bought me a jacket that was on **sale** at a local store.
Sea See	The discoverers sailed across the **sea** in huge ships. Everyone can **see** the performers when the stage is lit.
Soar Sore	When Davy lights the fuse, the rocket will **soar** high above us. Dana's throat was **sore** after all that screaming and cheering.
Straight Strait	The teacher used a ruler to make **straight** lines on the paper. A **strait** is a thin water passage joining two bodies of water.
Their They're There	The twins finally learned how to tie **their** own shoes. I stopped at the grocery, but **they're** out of navel oranges. (they are) We're on our way to the park; we'll eat lunch once we get **there**.
Threw Through	The quarterback **threw** the ball to Marco, so we stood to watch. Please don't walk **through** the house with those muddy shoes!
To Too Two	Make sure you unpack all of your clothes before you go **to** bed. The pie was **too** sweet for Angie. Bring soap and a towel, **too**. There was only one gas station last year, but now there are **two**.
Toad Towed	The ugly **toad** stared and croaked to let us know he saw us. The car had to be **towed** since one of the front tires was flat.
Waist Waste	She wore a leather fringed belt around her **waist**. If you cut the paper carefully, you won't **waste** any of it.
Weak Week	Rueben felt **weak** after the asthma attack. It will take about a **week** to build the new garage.
Weather Whether	The **weather** in Orlando, Florida is sunny and pleasant. Let me know **whether** or not I should get a ticket for you.
Who's Whose	Anyone **who's** going on the field trip needs a permission slip. (who is) Does anyone know **whose** backpack this is?
Would Wood	**Would** you like to go out to lunch? The trees are cut to harvest **wood** for building houses.
Your You're	Please invite **your** parents to our Family Fun Day. Call me if **you're** going to be late. (you are)

Level 6

Reading Comprehension

Answers to Lessons

	Lesson #1		Lesson #2
1	eager	1	C
2	(undaunted)	2	B
3	Getting there early gave her the freedom to visit with friends before the first bell.	3	Canada
4	D	4	Answers may vary. They use rainwater that is collected off rooftops and stored in tanks.
5	A	5	snorkeling
6	a distant planet	6	colossal
7	C	7	turquoise
8	appreciating	8	moisture
9	subdued	9	I can float effortlessly
10	unfamiliar	10	I safeguard my eyes by wearing sunglasses
11	unclear	11	the moisture in the atmosphere
12	shadowy	12	the country is an archipelago

Lesson #3		Lesson #4	
1	a model	1	D
2	to make the water more visible	2	C
3	none of these	3	B
4	Labor Day	4	A
5 - 12	**Across** 4. cycle 5. cloud 7. temperature 8. condensation **Down** 1. precipitation 2. ground 3. evaporation 6. vapor	5	C
		6	Back then, the U.S. military would not accept African American pilots.
		7	elected official surgeon
		8	Bessie's dream intensified
		9	George Coleman moved to Oklahoma
		10	her plane crashed
		11	she was the best manicurist in town
		12	cook

Lesson #5			Lesson #6	
1	D		1	There were no commercial flights at the time and no need for airline pilots.
2	fragile weak unstable		2	Bessie knew that she needed superior flying skills. Again, finding no willing teachers in Chicago, she sailed for France.
3	✓ racial discrimination ✓ gender discrimination		3	C
4	T		4	safe
5	F		5	predictable
6	D		6	horizontal
7	F		7	6
8	O		8	1
9	O		9	4
10 - 12	adventurous courageous Answers will vary. intelligent, hard-working, ambitious, determined, self-reliant, daring		10	5
			11	3
			12	2

Lesson #7		Lesson #8	
1	rainforest	1	B
2	B	2	A
3	habitat destruction disease	3	✓ quarrelsome at times ✓ determined to succeed
4	<u>The poison dart frog gets its name from the fact that its skin is poisonous, and this toxin was sometimes used by Native Americans on the tips of blow-dart weapons</u>.	4	timidly
5	eggs tadpole	5	independently
6	T	6	cooperative
7	diminutive	7	pail
8	poison	8	pale
9	home	9	waist
10	hunter	10	waste
11	sail	11	O
12	sale	12	O

Lesson #9		Lesson #10	
1	A	1	<u>He was told to keep the sheep together and under constant surveillance, as they grazed on the green hillsides above the village. The lad was instructed to alert the villagers at any sign of the prowling predator.</u>
2	C	2	Answers will vary.
3	E	3	A
4	C	4	(mischievous) (foolish) (troublesome)
5	E	5	calm
6	C	6	anxiety
7	E	7	marauder intruder
8	D	8	perplexed disgruntled confounded
9 - 12	Answers will vary. North Wind: arrogant, mischievous, annoying, immature, rude Sun: gentle, considerate, easy-going, modest, confident, capable	9	ruse
		10	sentinel
		11	reprimanded
		12	surveillance

Lesson #11	
1 - 12	**Across** 3. foreign 7. perplexed 9. vigilant 11. habitat 12. undaunted 13. obscure 16. unison 18. ruse 19. toxin 20. flimsy **Down** 1. surveillance 2. competitive 4. miniature 5. sentinel 6. archipelago 8. predator 10. marauder 14. colossal 15. vibrant 17. anxiety

Lesson #12	
1	B
2	C
3	D
4	a human
5	dove (bird)
6	strong
7	large
8	haphazardly
9	~~occupation~~
10	C
11	A
12	B

Lesson #13		Lesson #14	
1	B	**1**	B
2	H	**2**	elves in costumes
3	D	**3**	A
4	G	**4**	D
5	C	**5**	sleep
6	E	**6**	rain and dew
7 - 12	injudicious harmoniously measured amalgamated anticipation enumerate alienated triumphs saccharine seize	**7 - 12**	C D E F G B A

Lesson #15		Lesson #16	
1	D	1	his parents
2	editor	2	C
3	graphic designer	3	C
4	editor	4	C
5	graphic designer photographer	5	Then, he stepped over his father onto the platform. The car began its sluggish ascent, as Simon headed toward the exit ramp.
6	camera	6	The old coaster was made of wood
7	F	7	he refused to ride a roller coaster
8	O		
9	O	8 - 12	A A S S A S
10	most jobs require a college degree		
11	there are many different careers that require strong language skills		
12	The graphic designer works with both text and art		

Lesson #17		Lesson #18	
1	Italy	1	<u>Jamal had been born with cerebral palsy</u>.
2	all of these	2	B
3	C	3	D
4	Leon Battista Alberti Michelangelo Buanarroti	4	D
5	A	5	appreciative contented
6	C	6	<u>A person with cerebral palsy has trouble controlling his arms and legs</u>
7	D	7	speak
8	B	8	his grandma
9	A	9	Answers may vary. sure, confident, certain
10 - 12	C philosopher A grammarian D physicist B architect	10	(narrow-minded) <u>understanding</u>
		11	(demanding) <u>easy</u>
		12	(extraordinary) <u>commonplace</u>

	Lesson #19		Lesson #20
1	horseback riding	1	A
2	Answers will vary. improves balance, coordination, endurance; strengthens muscles; builds confidence, self-esteem, independence; it's fun	2	B
3	<u>tight pants, high black boots, and a funny looking hat</u>	3	D
4	A	4	Answers will vary. Example: Parents should be able to monitor internet use.
5	D	5	B
6	E	6	D
7	G	7	E
8	F	8	A
9	H	9	C
10	C	10	F
11	B	11	O
12	A	12	O

	Lesson #21			Lesson #22		
1	B		**1**	O		
2	more information about the other "teen traps" mentioned in the parenting magazine		**2**	O		
3	A		**3**	F		
4	C		**4**	F		
5	A		**5**	<u>talkative</u> <u>garrulous</u> <u>loquacious</u>		
6	C		**6**	<u>industrious</u> <u>lazy</u>		
7	<u>I use my computer time wisely</u>		**7**	they're		
8	<u>the cost of computer hardware</u>		**8**	their		
9	<u>I do my homework at the library</u>		**9**	There		
10	<u>I have privileges</u>		**10** - **12**	Supports Jeremy's Point of View: B, E		
11	through					
12	threw			Against Jeremy's Point of View: A, C, D, F, G		

Lesson #23		Lesson #24		
1	<u>A patch of crocuses, yellow like butternut squash</u>	1	(large)	tiny, small
2	the color of crocuses and the color of butternut squash	2	(acceptance)	rejection
3	moss and foam	3	(before)	after
4	C	4	(impossible)	possible
5	B	5	(fewer)	more
6	✓ Crocuses cuddle up... ✓ From the corner lawn...	6	(destroy)	save
7	frog	7	the creek water sounds	
8	bad-tempered irritable grumpy	8	P	
9	insatiable gluttonous ravenous	9	M	
10	road	10	P	
11	rowed	11	S	
12	rode	12	P	

	Lesson #25			Lesson #26
1	D		**1**	(Mary)
2	<u>chums</u> <u>pals</u> <u>friends</u>		**2**	<u>It shines like the face of the moon</u>.
3	C		**3**	*Margaret's expression* and *the face of the moon*
4	A		**4**	spring 1946 and fall 1999
5	C		**5**	B
6	D		**6**	~~disappointed~~
7	E		**7**	~~predict~~
8	A		**8**	Answers will vary. The pipecleaner doll had been there for over 50 years.
9	B		**9**	F
10	C		**10**	O
11	E		**11**	O
12	E		**12**	F

Lesson #27		Lesson #28	
1	unknown		**Across**
2	female		3. renaissance
3	A		5. seize
4	<u>Margaret introduced us</u>.		10. maneuvers
5	imaginary bad guys		11. simile
6	A		12. chaotic
7	<u>he thinks girls are not fun</u>		13. portfolio
8	<u>It's not polite to say someone has buck teeth</u>		15. burnished
			16. equestrian
9	<u>it's called "brush cut."</u>	**1**	17. diminutive
10	<u>I never see him there</u>	**-**	18. temperament
11	it's	**12**	19. ecstatic
			Down
			1. metaphor
			2. personification
			4. antagonist
12	its		6. memoir
			7. ambush
			8. cerebral
			9. endurance
			12. confidential
			14. gregarious

	Lesson #29		Lesson #30
1	at an amusement park	1	twister whirlwind cyclone
2	C	2	T
3	A	3	B
4	destructive powers	4	~~protected~~
5	D	5	~~balanced~~
6	With the image of the tornado barreling down on us eternally etched in my mind's eye, I can no longer recall how we got to safety. or Yet, to this day, when the sky grows dark, or when thunder sounds its menacing alarm, I am the first to cower in the basement.	6	warm moist air meets cool dry air
7	C	7	schools have periodic tornado drills
8	D	8	A tornado can be quite perilous
9	F	9	Today, fewer people are injured and killed during tornadoes.
10	E	10	O
11	B	11	F
12	A	12	O